God's Plan of Love

First Baptist, Jackson, Mississippi

Published by Innovo Publishing, LLC
www.innovopublishing.com
1-888-546-2111

Providing Full-Service Publishing Services for Christian Authors & Ministries:
Books, eBooks, Audiobooks, Music & Film

God's Plan of Love

Copyright © 2018 First Baptist, Jackson, Mississippi
All rights reserved.

No part of this publication may be reproduced, stored in a retrieval system, or transmitted in any form or by any means electronic, mechanical, photocopying, recording, or otherwise, without the prior written permission of the author.

Good News Translation® (Today's English Version)
Copyright © 1976 American Bible Society. All rights reserved.

Library of Congress Control Number: 2018942676
ISBN: 978-1-61314-400-8

Cover Design & Interior Layout: Innovo Publishing, LLC

Printed in the United States of America
U.S. Printing History
First Edition: 1984
Second Edition: 2003
Third Edition: 2016
Fourth Edition: 2018

Endorsements

"I loved these lessons for teaching the Bible to those who have never heard or studied the Bible and seeing their hearts open to God's truth. Written in a simple, easy-to-use, and easy-to-understand format and yet so profound."

—*Charlie and Nita, former teachers and directors of the Friend-to-Friend International Sunday School Department*

"*God's Plan of Love* and *God's Plan for Christian Living* were each written one Monday at a time, getting the lesson ready for the following Sunday. Countless hours were spent in prayer, writing, editing, and proofreading. They are not deep theological books, but simple, practical introductions to God's amazing love to and for those who have never heard!"

—*Becky, former director of the Friend-to-Friend International Ministry (week-day ministry and Sunday School Department) and one of the original authors*

"The request for an endorsement of these two books has stirred many long-ago memories of afternoons around a dining room table, of fervent prayers for guidance, of knowledge gleaned from lifetimes of sermons and Sunday School lessons, of a feeling of being carried along by a Power far beyond ourselves. But mostly my memories are of the people around that table and of the contributions each person made to our collaborative effort. We were simply writing 'next Sunday's lesson.' We never dreamed that those lessons could or would be used for many years and in many places. Praise God!"

—*Martha Jean, a long-time teacher in the Friend-to-Friend International Ministry and one of the original authors*

"*God's Plan of Love* and *God's Plan for Christian Living* were written by a group of dedicated Christian women. The lessons are well written and Christ centered. As a teacher for many years, I found the two books to be excellent teaching guides for me."

—*Clarice, a long-time and dedicated teacher in the Friend-to-Friend International Sunday School Department*

Acknowledgements

(1984)

First Baptist, Jackson, Mississippi, and the writers of this material express grateful acknowledgment to the American Bible Society for use of the Good News Bible, both text and illustrations, c. 1976.

We wish to thank Anand Michael from India who is a member of First Baptist, Jackson, Mississippi, and the International Sunday School. His contribution of time and effort in making attractive posters, vocabulary cards, and sentence strips for teaching aids was priceless.

First Baptist, Jackson, Mississippi, would also like to acknowledge the invaluable contributions of Mrs. Frances Smira, WMU Director, and Mr. David Roddy, Minister of Education. Without their help, this publication would not have been possible.

To the people who prayed for the writers/teachers and the writings, we give sincere and humble thanks.

INTERNATIONAL DEPARTMENT: First Baptist, Jackson, Mississippi

Mrs. Winfred (Becky) Lott, Director: 1980-2001

Teachers:	Associates:
Mrs. Joel (Martha Jean) Alvis	Dr. Joel E. Alvis
Mrs. Tom (Mercedes) Cleveland	Miss Fidelia Campbell
Mrs. Roy (Ann) Moore	Mrs. Roy (Georgie) Collum
Mrs. Herbert (Margaret) Price	Winfred B. Lott
Mrs. Robert (Rene) Sugg	Robert (Bob) Smira
	Mrs. Bob (Frances) Smira

Contents

Foreword xi
Foundational Biblical Truths xiii

Part I: God's Plan through the Bible

Lesson 1: *The Bible, Our Guidebook* 17
Lesson 2: *Why the Bible Was Written* 19
Lesson 3: *God, the Creator* 21
Lesson 4: *God Created Man* 23
Lesson 5: *God's Plan* 25
Lesson 6: *Man Chose His Way* 27
Lesson 7: *God Promised Life* 29
Lesson 8: *Noah Chose God's Way* 31
Lesson 9: *The Flood* 33
Lesson 10: *God's Plan for Abram* 35
Lesson 11: *Abraham: A Man of Faith* 38
Lesson 12: *God's Plan for Jacob* 41
Lesson 13: *Joseph Chose God's Way* 43
Lesson 14: *Joseph and His Brothers* 45
Lesson 15: *Joseph: A Part of God's Plan* 47
Lesson 16: *God's People in Egypt* 49
Lesson 17: *God Called Moses* 53
Lesson 18: *God's Plan for Moses* 56
Lesson 19: *God's Plan to Free the Israelites* 59
Lesson 20: *The Israelites Chose God's Plan* 62
Lesson 21: *God Gave the Ten Commandments* 66
Lesson 22: *The Journey to the Promised Land* 69
Lesson 23: *Joshua, the New Leader of the Israelites* 72

Contents

Lesson 24: *Ruth in God's Plan* 75
Lesson 25: *God Gave Kings to Israel* 77
Lesson 26: *David's Sin and God's Forgiveness* 79
Lesson 27: *Psalms, the Song and Prayer Book of the Bible* 82
Lesson 28: *God Fulfilled His Promises* 84
Lesson 29: *God Fulfilled His Promises (Continued)* 87
Lesson 30: *God Continues His Plan in the New Testament* 89
Lesson 31: *Mary Chose God's Plan* 90
Lesson 32: *The Birth of Jesus* 92
Lesson 33: *The Christmas Story* 94

Part II: Jesus: All God and All Man

Lesson 34: *Jesus, All God and All Man* 96
Lesson 35: *The Baptism of Jesus* 98
Lesson 36: *The Temptation of Jesus* 100
Lesson 37: *Why Jesus Came* 102
Lesson 38: *The I AMs of Jesus* 104
Lesson 39: *I Am the Way, the Truth, and the Life* 106
Lesson 40: *God Is ALL Powerful* 108
Lesson 41: *God Cares* 110
Lesson 42: *God Forgives* 112
Lesson 43: *God Loves* 114
Lesson 44: *God Loves All People* 116
Lesson 45: *God Loves Bad People* 118
Lesson 46: *God Loves Good People* 120
Lesson 47: *God Loves Women and Children* 122

Part III: Jesus Teaches Christians How to Live

Lesson 48: *Love God* 127
Lesson 49: *Love People* 129
Lesson 50: *Tell People* 131

Part IV: Jesus' Death and Resurrection Bring Life in All Its Fullness

Lesson 51: *Jesus' Special Supper with His Friends*...........135
Lesson 52: *Jesus in the Garden of Gethsemane*...........137
Lesson 53: *Jesus' Trial*...........139
Lesson 54: *Jesus' Death on the Cross*...........143
Lesson 55: *The Lord Is Risen*...........147
Lesson 56: *Jesus' Last Days on Earth*...........149
Lesson 57: *The Promise of the Holy Spirit*...........152
Lesson 58: *The Coming of the Holy Spirit*...........154
Lesson 59: *God's Plan to Love People*...........156
Lesson 60: *God's Plan for People to Love God*...........159
Lesson 61: *God's Plan: Life in All Its Fullness*...........161

Part V: The People God Chose to Start and Build His Church

Lesson 62: *The Beginning of the Church*...........169
Lesson 63: *The Beginning of the Church (Continued)*...........171
Lesson 64: *Peter's Call and Answer*...........173
Lesson 65: *Peter's Denial and God's Forgiveness*...........175
Lesson 66: *Peter Began His Assignment to Help Build the Church*...........177
Lesson 67: *Peter Continued His Assignment to Help Build the Church*...........179
Lesson 68: *Cornelius Chose to Be a Part of God's Church*...........181
Lesson 69: *Stephen Gave His Life to Help Build the Church*...........184
Lesson 70: *Philip Helped to Build the Church in Many Places*...........187
Lesson 71: *Saul: A Very Special Jew*...........190
Lesson 72: *Saul: A New Person in Christ*...........192
Lesson 73: *Paul: God's Missionary to the World*...........195
Lesson 74: *Paul: God's Helper with Many Churches*...........198
Lesson 75: *Paul Told How to Be Saved from Eternal Death to Eternal Life*...........200
Lesson 76: *Paul Told Christians How to Praise God*...........203
Lesson 77: *Paul Described Christian Love*...........205
Lesson 78: *Paul Told Christians How to Live a Life in God's Service*...........207

Contents

    Lesson 79: *Paul Told That the Church Is the Body of Christ—All the Believers in Jesus Christ* 210

    Lesson 80: *Jesus Is Coming Again* 212

Part VI: The Bible Teaches Us about Prayer

    Lesson 81: *What Is Prayer?* 217

    Lesson 82: *Why Do People Pray?* 219

    Lesson 83: *How Do People Pray?* 222

    Lesson 84: *What Are Some Ways to Pray?* 224

    Lesson 85: *Does God Answer Prayer?* 226

    Lesson 86: *What Helps Christians Pray?* 228

    Lesson 87: *How Do I Pray?* 230

Foreword

The Bible study material included in *God's Plan of Love* and *God's Plan for Christian Living* was prepared initially for use with international adults* in a Sunday school setting. It was written for people with a limited knowledge of English. No background knowledge of the Bible was assumed.

Two principles were followed in writing the lessons: One was to present the thread of redemption from the creation of the world through the death, burial, resurrection, and ascension of Jesus, including two lessons giving the plan of salvation. The thread of redemption was also carried through the beginning of the church and the second coming of Jesus. The lessons stress the importance of choosing God's way (making a decision of faith in Jesus) and obedience.

The other principle in both volumes was to replace theological terms with simple, everyday words to teach spiritual truths.

This material was written as basic statements to be used as a guide, by which lessons could be prepared to teach people at different levels of English proficiency. Understanding on the part of the students was of more importance than strict adherence to accepted outline procedure.

Each lesson may be easily divided into shorter lessons when repetition and simplification are needed. On the other hand, each lesson, or portions thereof, can be taken to a more advanced English level by using the Bible itself to expand the details of the truth being taught, to raise the language level, and to introduce deeper concepts that might be needed.

The initial teaching of this material began in May 1984, with a natural progression of study planned to teach the birth of Jesus at Christmas and the death, burial, and resurrection during the Easter season. However, each of these special lessons can be taught whenever they occur in your schedule of classes or saved for Christmas and Easter, respectively.

The Good News Bible, c. 1976, was used as a textbook. Illustrations from the Good News Bible, c. 1976, were included in the original writing.

In this 2018 edition of *God's Plan of Love* and *God's Plan for Christian Living*, the quotations from the Good News Bible have been retained with spaces after each quotation for page numbers to be inserted to help those students who may be unfamiliar with the Bible. You

Foreword

will need to explain the variety of translations available today and why you have chosen the version you prefer to use.

The original authors of these lessons dedicated them to the glory of God. Others who have taught these lessons for more than thirty years pray that you who teach them today will be able to adapt and use them to bring many people to "the throne of grace" and for the glory of the God and Father of our Lord Jesus.

---

* Beyond the express purpose for which *God's Plan of Love* and *God's Plan for Christian Living* were written—that is, for limited English speakers—we commend these lessons to all Bible teachers as suitable for study by native English speakers. New believers in Jesus Christ as well as Christians who may not be thoroughly familiar with the Bible would benefit greatly from studying the chronological presentation of the highlights of the Bible in simple English.

Foundational Biblical Truths

1. **God is love.**

    1 John 4:10, 16b (page _____ in the New Testament): This is what love is: it is not that we have loved God, but that He loved us and sent His Son to be the means by which our sins are forgiven . . . God is love and whoever lives in love, lives in union with God and God lives in union with him.

    1 John 4:8 (page _____ in the New Testament): Whoever does not love, does not know God, for God is love.

2. **God had a plan to reveal His love.**

    John 3:16 (page _____ in the New Testament): For God loved the world so much that He gave His only Son, so that everyone who believes in Him may not die but have eternal life.

3. **God carried out His plan of love through people.**

    Ephesians 1:4-5 (page _____ in the New Testament): Even before the world was made, God had already chosen us to be His through our union with Christ, so that we would be holy and without fault before Him. Because of His love God had already decided that through Jesus Christ He would make us His sons-this was His pleasure and purpose.

    Some of the people God used were Adam and Eve, Noah, Abraham, Joseph, Moses, Ruth, David, Isaiah, Jesus, Peter, Cornelius, Stephen, Philip, and Paul.

4. **God made man free to choose.**

    Genesis 2:16-17 (page _____ in the Old Testament): He told him, "You may eat the fruit of any tree in the garden, except the tree that gives knowledge of what is good and what is bad."

Foundational Biblical Truths

5. **Sin is choosing my own way.**

    Isaiah 53:6 (page _____ in the Old Testament): All of us are like sheep that were lost, each of us going his own way. But the LORD made the punishment fall on Him, the punishment all of us deserved.

6. **God forgives sin and the sinner.**

    Colossians 2:13b-14 (page _____ in the New Testament): But God has now brought you to life with Christ. God forgave us all our sins; He canceled the unfavorable record of our debts with its binding rules and did away with it completely by nailing it to the cross.

    i. God erases sin.
       Psalm 103:12 (page _____ in the Old Testament): As far as the east is from the west, so far did He remove our sins from us.

    ii. God makes clean.
       Isaiah 1:18b (page _____ in the Old Testament): You are stained red with sin, but I will wash you as clean as snow.

    iii. God makes right.
       Romans 3:20, 22a (page _____ in the New Testament): For no one is put right in God's sight by doing what the Law requires; what the Law does is to make man know that he has sinned….God puts people right through their faith in Jesus Christ.

7. **Salvation is choosing God's way.**

    Acts 16:31 (page _____ in the New Testament): Believe in the Lord Jesus and you will be saved.

    John 1:12 (page _____ in the New Testament): Some, however, did receive Him and believed in Him; so He gave them the right to become God's children.

    Romans 10:13 (page _____ in the New Testament): As the Scripture says, "Everyone who calls out to the Lord for help will be saved."

    Ephesians 2:8-9 (page _____ in the New Testament): For it is by God's grace that you have been saved through faith. It is not the result of your own efforts, but God's gift, so that no one can boast about it.

Part I:

God's Plan through the Bible

Lesson 1

The Bible, Our Guidebook

1. **The Bible is the Holy Book for Christians.**

2. **The Bible has many books.**

3. **The Bible is a letter from God to man. God told men what to write in the Bible.**

   2 Timothy 3:16 (page _____ in the New Testament): All Scripture is inspired by God and is useful for teaching the truth, rebuking error, correcting faults, and giving instruction for right living.

4. **The message of the Bible is God's love for man. God says, "I love you."**

5. **The Bible is a lamp.**

   Psalm 119:105 (page _____ in the Old Testament): Your word is a lamp to guide me and a light for my path.

   A flashlight shows us where to walk on a dark street. A lamp gives light in a dark room.

7. **The Bible is a road map.**

   Isaiah 58:11 (page _____ in the Old Testament): "And I will always guide you and satisfy you with good things. I will keep you strong and well. You will be like a garden that has plenty of water, like a spring of water that never goes dry."

God's Plan of Love

The Bible shows the right way for us to live.

> Fill the blank spaces in the sentences below with one of these words:

Bible   road map   God   "I love you"   lamp

1. The Bible is a letter from _____.

2. God says _____.

3. The Bible is a _____.

4. The Bible is a _____.

5. The _____ tells us what to do and how to live.

Lesson 2

Why the Bible Was Written

1. **God told men what to write in the Bible.**

    2 Timothy 3:16 (page _____ in the New Testament): All Scripture is inspired by God and is useful for teaching the truth, rebuking error, correcting faults and giving instruction for right living.

2. **God used forty men over a period of 1,500 years to write the Bible.**

3. **The Bible was written in the language of the people who lived at that time.**

4. **The Bible is being translated into the languages of all the people of the world.**

    Isaiah 55:11 (page _____ in the Old Testament): So also will be the word that I speak— it will not fail to do what I plan for it; it will do everything I send it to do.

5. **The Bible has two parts: The Old Testament and the New Testament.**

    Genesis 1:1a (page _____ in the Old Testament): In the beginning, when God created the universe.

    Matthew 1:1 (page _____ in the New Testament): This is the list of ancestors of Jesus Christ, a descendant of David, who was a descendant of Abraham.

God's Plan of Love

6. All of the Bible tells one story. It is the story of God's love through His Son, Jesus.

John 3:16 (page _____ in the New Testament): For God loved the world so much that He gave His only Son, so that everyone who believes in Him may not die but have eternal life.

> Draw a line under the word which makes each sentence complete.
> Write the word in the blank space:

1. God told _____ men to write the Bible.   **50   100   40**

2. _____ told men what to write.   **Jesus God   Bible**

3. The Bible has _____ parts.   **4   8   2**

4. The _____ Testament tells the life of Jesus.   **New   Old   Bible**

5. The Bible tells the story of God's _____ through His Son, Jesus.   **Love New   Bible**

Part I: God's Plan through the Bible

Lesson 3

God, the Creator

1. **All the Bible tells one story. It is the story of God's love through His Son, Jesus.**

2. **The story begins in the first book of the Bible, the book of Genesis.**

    Genesis 1:1-2 (page _____ in the Old Testament): In the beginning when God created the universe, the earth was formless and desolate.

3. **Genesis tells us that God made the world.**

4. **God made man.**

    Genesis 2:7 (page _____ in the Old Testament): Then the Lord God took some soil from the ground and formed a man out of it; He breathed life-giving breath into his nostrils and the man began to live.

5. **All the Bible tells that God had a plan to love people and for people to love Him.**

    John 3:16 (page _____ in the New Testament): For God loved the world so much that He gave His only Son, so that everyone who believes in Him may not die but have eternal life.

God's Plan of Love

Fill the blank spaces in the sentences below with one of these words:

plan **Bible** **world** **Genesis** **God's**

1. All the _____ tells one story.

2. It is the story of _____ love through His Son, Jesus.

3. God made the _____.

4. The first book in the Bible is _____.

5. God has a _____ to love people and for people to love Him.

Some letters are missing in John 3:16. Fill in the missing letters:

F___r G___d l___ved th___ w___rld s___ m___ch th___t H__ g___ve H___s o___ly S___n, s___ th___t ___v___ryone wh___ b___li___ves ___n H___m m___y n___t d___e b___t h___ve ___ter___al l___fe.

Lesson 4

God Created Man

1. **The Bible tells us that God made the world.**

    i. God made the day and night: Genesis 1:3-5 (page _____ in the Old Testament).

    ii. God made the sky: Genesis 1:6-8 (page _____ in the Old Testament).

    iii. God made the earth, sea, and all kinds of plants: Genesis 1:9-13 (page _____ in the Old Testament).

    iv. God made the sun, moon, and stars: Genesis 1:14-19 (page _____ in the Old Testament).

    v. God made the animals and birds: Genesis 1:20-23 (page _____ in the Old Testament).

    vi. God made the land animals: Genesis 1:24-25 (page _____ in the Old Testament).

2. **The Bible tells us that God made man.**

    Genesis 2:7 (page _____ in the Old Testament): Then the Lord God took some soil from the ground and formed a man out of it; He breathed life-giving breath into his nostrils and the man began to live.

3. **The Bible tells us that God finished His creation.**

    Genesis 2:2 (page _____ in the Old Testament): By the seventh day God finished what He had been doing and stopped working.

God's Plan of Love

4. The Bible tells us that God loves us.

John 3:16 (page _____ in the New Testament)

1 John 4:10 (page _____ in the New Testament): This is what love is: it is not that we have loved God, but that He loved us and sent His Son to be the means by which our sins are forgiven.

> Fill the blank spaces in the sentences below with one of these words:

world   earth   creation   moon   birds

man   sea   animals   everyone   plants   day

1. God made all things. He created the _____.

2. He created the _____.

3. God loves _____.

4. God finished His _____.

5. God made the _____

6. God made the _____.

7. God made the _____.

8. God made the _____.

9. God made the _____.

10. God made the _____.

11. Then God made _____.

Lesson 5

God's Plan

1. **God made man different from other creation. God made man like Himself. He made man free to choose.**

   Genesis 1:27 (page _____ in the Old Testament): So God created human beings, making them to be like Himself.

2. **Everything God made was good.**

   Genesis 1:31 (page _____ in the Old Testament): God looked at everything He had made, and He was very pleased.

3. **God made a special home for man. He named it the Garden of Eden.**

   Genesis 2:8 (page _____ in the Old Testament): Then the LORD God planted a garden in Eden, in the East, and there He put the man He had formed.

4. **God had a plan to love people and for people to love God.**

   Genesis 2:15-17 (page _____ in the Old Testament): Then the LORD God placed the man in the Garden of Eden to cultivate it and guard it. He told him, "You may eat the fruit of any tree in the garden, except the tree that gives knowledge of what is good and what is bad. You must not eat the fruit of that tree; if you do, you will die the same day."

God's Plan of Love

> God's plan was for God and man to be together:
>
> to walk together,
>
> to talk together,
>
> to be friends together.

> DID YOU KNOW? Here are some facts about the Bible. As you read each statement, decide whether it tells something you did not know before. If it does, put a check mark on the line in front of the statement. When you have finished, look back over the list. How many new things did you discover?

_____ **The Bible is the Word of God.**

_____ **The Bible is many books in one. The Bible has sixty-six books in it.**

_____ **The Bible has two main parts: The Old Testament and the New Testament.**

_____ **The Old Testament has thirty-nine books.**

_____ **The New Testament has twenty-seven books.**

_____ **Under the inspiration (leadership) of God, about forty men wrote various parts of the Bible.**

_____ **The Bible was written over a period of about fifteen hundred years.**

_____ **Most of the Old Testament was written in the Hebrew language.**

_____ **Greek was the language of the New Testament.**

_____ **The writers of the Bible wrote the message God wanted them to write. They wrote as they were inspired (led) by God.**

_____ **The Bible tells us about God's plan to send Jesus to earth.**

_____ **The Bible tells us about God's plan for me—what He wants me to be and to do.**

_____ **The Bible tells us of real people who lived long ago in the part of the world we now call the Middle East.**

Lesson 6

Man Chose His Way

God's plan was for God and man to be together:

to walk together, to talk together,

to be friends together.

1. **Man did not choose God's plan.**

   Genesis 3:6 (page _____ in the Old Testament): The woman saw how beautiful the tree was and how good its fruit would be to eat, and she thought how wonderful it would be to become wise. So she took some of the fruit and ate it. Then she gave some to her husband, and he ate also.

2. **Sin came into the world. Sin is choosing my own way instead of God's way.**

   Isaiah 53:6 (page _____ in the Old Testament): All of us were like sheep that were lost, each of us going his own way. But the LORD made the punishment fall on Him, the punishment all of us deserved.

3. **Sin brings death. Death is separation from God.**

   Genesis 2:15-17 (page _____ in the Old Testament): Then the LORD God placed the man in the Garden of Eden to cultivate and guard it. He told him, "You may eat the fruit of any tree in the garden except the tree that gives knowledge of what is good and what is bad. You must not eat the fruit of that tree; if you do, you will die the same day."

   Genesis 3:22-23 (page _____ in the Old Testament): Then the LORD God said, "Now the man has become like one of us and has knowledge of what is good and what is bad. He must not be allowed to eat fruit from the tree of life and live forever." So the LORD God sent him out of the Garden of Eden, and made him cultivate the soil from which he had been formed.

God's Plan of Love

4. **God's plan brings life.**

   i. God promised Jesus.

   Genesis 3:15b (page _____ in the Old Testament): Her offspring will crush your head, and you will bite their heel.

   ii. Jesus came.

   Luke 2:11 (page _____ in the New Testament): This very day in David's town your Saviour was born—Christ the Lord.

   iii. Jesus brings life.

   John 3:16 (page _____ in the New Testament): For God loved the world so much that He gave His only Son, so that everyone who believes in Him may not die but have eternal life.

Fill the blank spaces in the sentences below with one of these words:

home   life   man   God's way   everything

people   creation   plan   Garden of Eden

1. God made man different from other _____.

2. _____ God made was good.

3. God made a special _____ for man.

4. He named it the _____.

5. God had a _____ to love people and for _____ to love Him.

6. _____ did not choose God's way.

7. Sin is going my way instead of _____.

8. God's plan brings _____.

Lesson 7

God Promised Life

God made man different from His other creation.

God made man like Himself.

Genesis 1:27 (page _____ in the Old Testament): So God created human beings, making them to be like Himself. He created them male and female.

God made man free to choose.

Genesis 2:16-17 (page _____ in the Old Testament): He told him, "You may eat the fruit of any tree in the garden, except the tree that gives knowledge of what is good and what is bad. You must not eat the fruit of that tree; if you do you will die the same day."

Man chose his own way. Choosing my own way is sin.

Sin brings death.

Romans 6:23 (page _____ in the New Testament): For sin pays its wage—death; but God's free gift is eternal life in union with Christ Jesus our Lord.

1. **God dealt with sin.**

    i. Man chose to turn from God.

    Genesis 3:8 (page _____ in the Old Testament): That evening they heard the LORD God walking in the garden, and they hid from Him among the trees.

    ii. Separation from God is death.

    Romans 5:12 (page _____ in the New Testament): Sin came into the world by one man, and his sin brought death with it. As a result, death has spread to the whole human race because everyone has sinned.

God's Plan of Love

    iii. God dealt with man's choice.

    Genesis 3:23 (page _____ in the Old Testament): So the LORD God sent him out of the Garden of Eden and made him cultivate the soil from which he had been formed.

2. **God promised life.**

    Genesis 3:15b (page _____ in the Old Testament): Her offspring will crush your head, and you will bite their heel.

    i. God loves us.

    1 John 4:10 (page _____ in the New Testament): This is what love is: it is not that we have loved God, but that He loved us and sent His Son to be the means by which our sins are forgiven.

    ii. God gives life.

    John 3:16 (page _____ in the New Testament): For God loved the world so much that He gave His only Son, so that everyone who believes in Him may not die but have eternal life.

Fill the blank spaces in the sentences below with one of these words:

Loves	**God**	**life**	**different**	**chose**

1. God made man _____ from other creation.

2. Man _____ to turn from God.

3. Separation from _____ means death.

4. God _____ us.

5. God gives _____.

Lesson 8

Noah Chose God's Way

God had a plan to love all people and for all people to love Him.

1 John 4:10 (page _____ in the New Testament): This is what love is: it is not that we have loved God, but that He loved us and sent His Son to be the means by which our sins are forgiven.

Man did not choose God's plan. Man chose his own way.

Isaiah 53:6a (page _____ in the Old Testament): All of us were like sheep that were lost, each of us going his own way.

1. **God saw man's sin.**

   Genesis 6:5-7 (page _____ in the Old Testament): When the LORD saw how wicked everyone on earth was and how evil their thoughts were all the time, He was sorry that He had ever made them and put them on the earth. He was so filled with regret that He said, "I will wipe out these people I have created, and also the animals and the birds, because I am sorry that I made any of them."

2. **God had a plan to destroy the world.**

   Genesis 6:17 (page _____ in the Old Testament): "I am going to send a flood on the earth to destroy every living being. Everything on the earth will die."

3. **God was pleased with Noah.**

   Genesis 6:8, l0b (page _____ in the Old Testament): But the LORD was pleased with Noah. . . . He lived in fellowship with God.

God's Plan of Love

4. **God had a plan to save Noah and his family.**

    Genesis 6:18 (page _____ in the Old Testament): "But I will make a covenant with you. Go into the boat with your wife, your sons, and their wives."

5. **God destroyed the world with a flood.**

    Genesis 7:23a (page _____ in Old Testament): The LORD destroyed all living beings on the earth-human beings, animals, and birds.

6. **God saved Noah and his family.**

    Genesis 7:23b (page _____ in the Old Testament): The only ones left were Noah and those who were with him in the boat.

7. **God kept His promise to Noah.**

    Genesis 9:13-17 (page _____ in the Old Testament): "I am putting My bow in the clouds. It will be the sign of My covenant with the world. Whenever I cover the sky with clouds and the rainbow appears, I will remember My promise to you and to all the animals that a flood will never again destroy all living beings. When the rainbow appears in the clouds, I will see it and remember the everlasting covenant between Me and all living beings on earth. That is the sign of the promise which I am making to all living beings."

8. **God keeps His promise today.**

    John 3:16 (page _____ in the New Testament): For God loved the world so much that He gave His only son, so that everyone who believes in Him may not die but have eternal life.

Lesson 9

The Flood

1. **God is love.**

    1 John 4:8 (page _____ in the New Testament): Whoever does not love does not know God, for God is love.

    1 John 4:10, 16b (page _____ in the New Testament): This is what love is: it is not that we have loved God, but that He loved us and sent His Son to be the means by which our sins are forgiven. . . . God is love.

2. **God had a plan to love people and for people to love Him.**

    Genesis 1:27-29 (page _____ in the Old Testament): So God created human beings, making them to be like Himself. He created them male and female, blessed them, and said, "Have many children, so that your descendants will live all over the earth and bring it under their control. I am putting you in charge of the fish, the birds, and all the wild animals. I have provided all kinds of grain and all kinds of fruit for you to eat."

3. **Man chose his own way.**

    Genesis 6:5-7 (page _____ in the Old Testament): When the LORD saw how wicked everyone on earth was and how evil their thoughts were all the time, He was sorry that He had ever made them and put them on the earth. He was so filled with regret that He said, "I will wipe out these people I have created, and also the animals and the birds, because I am sorry that I made any of them."

God's Plan of Love

    i. God had a plan to destroy the world.

Genesis 6:17 (page _____ in the Old Testament): "I am going to send a flood on the earth to destroy every living being. Everything on the earth will die."

    ii. God was pleased with Noah.

Genesis 6:8, 10b (page _____ in the Old Testament): But the LORD was pleased with Noah. . . . He lived in fellowship with God.

    iii. God had a plan to save Noah and his family.

Genesis 6:18 (page _____ in the Old Testament): "But I will make a covenant with you. Go into the boat with your wife, your sons, and their wives."

    iv. God destroyed the world with a flood.

Genesis 7:23a (page _____ in the Old Testament): The LORD destroyed all living beings on the earth.

    v. God saved Noah and his family.

Genesis 7:23b (page _____ in the Old Testament): The only ones left were Noah and those who were with him in the boat.

    vi. God kept His promise to Noah.

Genesis 9:13-17 (page _____ in the Old Testament): "I am putting My bow in the clouds. It will be the sign of My covenant with the world. Whenever I cover the sky with clouds and the rainbow appears, I will remember My promise to you and to all the animals that a flood will never again destroy all living beings. When the rainbow appears in the clouds, I will see it and remember the everlasting covenant between Me and all living beings on earth. That is the sign of the promise which I am making to all living beings."

Genesis 8:22 (page _____ in the Old Testament): As long as the world exists, there will be a time for planting and a time for harvest. There will always be cold and heat, summer and winter, day and night.

4. God keeps His promise today.

John 3:16 (page _____ in the New Testament): For God loved the world so much that He gave His only Son, so that everyone who believes in Him may not die but have eternal life.

Lesson 10

God's Plan for Abram

GOD kept His promise to Noah.

Genesis 9:13-17 (page _____ in the Old Testament): "I am putting my bow in the clouds. It will be the sign of my covenant with the world. Whenever I cover the sky with clouds and the rainbow appears, I will remember my promise to you and all the animals that a flood will never again destroy all living beings. When the rainbow appears in the clouds, I will see it and remember the everlasting covenant between me and all living beings on earth. That is the sign of the promise which I am making to all living beings."

Genesis 8:22 (page _____ in the Old Testament): "As long as the world exists, there will be a time for planting and a time for harvest. There will always be cold and heat, summer and winter, day and night."

GOD has kept His promises through all of the Bible, and He keeps His promises to us today.

John 3:16 (page _____ in the New Testament): For God loved the world so much that He gave His only Son, so that everyone who believes in Him may not die but have eternal life.

FAITH is believing and trusting God.

FAITH is taking God at His word.

Hebrews 11:1, 2, 3, 6, 7a-b (page _____ in the New Testament): To have faith is to be sure of the things we hope for, to be certain of the things we cannot see. It was by their faith that people of ancient times won God's approval. It is by faith that we understand that the universe was created by God's word, so that what can be seen was made out of what cannot be seen. . . . No one can please God without faith, for whoever comes to

God's Plan of Love

God must have faith that God exists and rewards those who seek Him. It was faith that made Noah hear God's warnings about things in the future that he could not see. He obeyed God and built a boat in which he and his family were saved.

1. **God chose Abram to be a part of His plan.**

   Genesis 12:1 (page _____ in the Old Testament): The LORD said to Abram, "Leave your country, your relatives, and your father's home, and go to a land that I am going to show you."

2. **God made a covenant with Abram.**

   Genesis 12:2-3 (page _____ in the Old Testament): "I will give you many descendants, and they will become a great nation. I will bless you and make your name famous, so that you will be a blessing. I will bless those who bless you, but I will curse those who curse you. And through you I will bless all the nations."

3. **Abram chose God's way.**

   Genesis 12:4 (page _____ in the Old Testament): When Abram was seventy-five years old, he started out from Haran, as the LORD had told him to do; and Lot went with him.

4. **Abram went where God led.**

   Genesis 12:5-9 (page _____ in the Old Testament): Abram took his wife Sarai, his nephew Lot, and all the wealth and all the slaves they had acquired in Haran, and they started out for the land of Canaan. When they arrived in Canaan, Abram traveled through the land until he came to the sacred tree of Moreh, the holy place at Shechem. (At that time the Canaanites were still living in the land.) The LORD appeared to Abram and said to him, "This is the country that I am going to give to your descendants." Then Abram built an altar there to the LORD, who had appeared to him. After that, he moved on south to the hill country east of the city of Bethel and set up his camp between Bethel on the west and Ai on the east. There also he built an altar and worshiped the LORD. Then he moved on from place to place, going toward the southern pan of Canaan.

5. **Abram sinned.**

   Genesis 12:10-20 (page _____ in the Old Testament): But there was famine in Canaan, and it was so bad that Abram went farther south to Egypt, to live there for a while. When he was about to cross the border into Egypt, he said to his wife Sarai, "You are a beautiful woman. When the Egyptians see you, they will assume that you are my wife, and so they will kill me and let you live. Tell them that you are my sister; then because of you they will let me live and treat me well." When he crossed the border into Egypt, the Egyptians did see that his wife was beautiful. Some of the court officials saw her and told the king how beautiful she was; so she was taken to his palace. Because of her the king treated Abram well and gave him flocks of sheep and goats, cattle, donkeys, slaves, and camels. But because the king had taken Sarai, the LORD sent terrible diseases on him and on the people of his palace. Then the king sent for Abram and asked him, "What have you done to me? Why didn't you tell me that she was your wife? Why did you say that she was your sister, and let me take her as my wife? Here is your wife; take her and get out." The king gave orders to his men, so they took Abram and put him out of the country, together with his wife and everything he owned.

6. **Abram trusted in God.**

   Genesis 15:6 (page _____ in the Old Testament): Abram put his trust in the LORD, and because of this the LORD was pleased with him and accepted him.

7. **Abram's name was changed to Abraham.**

   Genesis 17:5-6 (page _____ in the Old Testament): "Your name will no longer be Abram, but Abraham, because I am making you the ancestor of many nations. I will give you many descendants, and some of them will be kings. You will have so many descendants that they will become nations."

8. **God renewed His promise to Abraham.**

   Genesis 17:7 (page _____ in the Old Testament): "I will keep my promise to you and to your descendants in future generations as an everlasting covenant. I will be your God and the God of your descendants."

Use these words to complete the following verse:

eternal   **die**   **God**   **believes**

world   **gave**   **Son**   **everyone**

For _____ loved the _____ so much that He _____ his only _____, so that _____ who _____ in Him may not _____ but have _____ life. (John 3:16)

Lesson 11

Abraham: A Man of Faith

God chose Abraham to be a part of His plan.

Genesis 12:1 (page _____ in the Old Testament): The LORD spoke to Abram, "Leave your country, your relatives, and your father's home, and go to a land that I am going to show you."

Abraham trusted in God.

Genesis 15:6 (page _____ in the Old Testament): Abram put his trust in the LORD, and because of this the LORD was pleased with him and accepted him.

God renewed His promise to Abraham.

Genesis 17:7 (page _____ in the Old Testament): "I will keep my promise to you and to your descendants in future generations as an everlasting covenant. I will be your God and the God of your descendants. "

1. **God promised Abraham a son.**

   Genesis 17:15-16 (page _____ in the Old Testament): God said to Abraham, "You must no longer call your wife Sarai; from now on her name is Sarah. I will bless her, and I will give you a son by her. I will bless her, and she will become the mother of nations, and there will be kings among her descendants."

2. **God kept His promise to Abraham.**

   Genesis 21:1-3 (page _____ in the Old Testament): The LORD blessed Sarah, as He had promised, and she became pregnant and bore a son to Abraham when he was old. The boy was born at the time God had said he would be born. Abraham named him Isaac.

Part I: God's Plan through the Bible

3. **God tested Abraham.**

   Genesis 22:1-2 (page _____ in the Old Testament): Some time later God tested Abraham; He called to him, "Abraham!" And Abraham answered, "Yes, here I am!" "Take your son," God said, "your only son, Isaac, whom you love so much, and go to the land of Moriah. There on a mountain that I will show you, offer him as a sacrifice to me."

4. **Abraham offered his son.**

   Genesis 22:3-10 (page _____ in the Old Testament): Early the next morning Abraham cut some wood for the sacrifice, loaded his donkey, and took Isaac and two servants with him. They started out for the place that God had told him about. On the third day Abraham saw the place in the distance. Then he said to the servants, "Stay here with the donkey. The boy and I will go over there and worship, and then we will come back to you." Abraham made Isaac carry the wood for the sacrifice, and he himself carried a knife and live coals for starting the fire. As they walked along together, Isaac spoke up, "Father!" He answered, "Yes, my son?" Isaac asked, "I see that you have the coals and the wood, but where is the lamb for the sacrifice?" Abraham answered, "God himself will provide one." And the two of them walked on together. When they came to the place which God had told him about, Abraham built an altar and arranged the wood on it. He tied up his son and placed him on the altar, on top of the wood. Then he picked up the knife to kill him.

5. **God saved Abraham's son.**

   Genesis 22:11-14 (page _____ in the Old Testament): But the angel of the LORD called to him from heaven, "Abraham, Abraham!" He answered, "Yes, here I am." "Don't hurt the boy or do anything to him," he said. "Now I know that you honor and obey God, because you have not kept back your only son from him." Abraham looked around and saw a ram caught in a bush by its hams. He went and got it and offered it as a burnt offering instead of his son. Abraham named that place "The LORD Provides." And even today people say, "On the LORD'S mountain He provides."

6. **God offered His Son.**

   Hebrews 9:28a (page _____ in the New Testament): In the same manner Christ also was offered in sacrifice once to take away the sins of many.

God's Plan of Love

7. God did not save His Son.

Luke 23:33 (page _____ in the New Testament): When they came to the place called The Skull, they crucified Jesus there, and the two criminals, one on His right and the other on His left.

8. God saves us through His Son.

1 John 4:9 (page _____ in the New Testament): And God showed His love for us by sending His only Son into the world, so that we might have life through Him.

John 3:16 (page _____ in the New Testament): For God loved the world so much that He gave His only Son, so that everyone who believes in Him may not die but have eternal life.

Fill the blank spaces in the sentences below with one of these words:

Abraham   Isaac   Canaan   Sarah   ram   altar   Genesis

1. God led Abraham to the land of _____.

2. _____ was Abraham's wife.

3. The book in the Bible which tells the story of Abraham is _____.

4. Abraham built an _____ and worshiped God.

5. Abraham named his beloved son _____.

6. God chose _____ to start a new nation.

7. God provided a _____ for Abraham to use as a burnt offering.

Lesson 12

God's Plan for Jacob

1. **Through Isaac, Abraham's son, the promises of God were passed down to Jacob.**

   Genesis 26:23-25a (page _____ in the Old Testament): Isaac left and went to Beersheba. That night the LORD appeared to him and said, "I am the God of your father Abraham. Do not be afraid; I am with you. I will bless you and give you many descendants because of My promise to My servant Abraham." Isaac built an altar there and worshiped the LORD.

   Genesis 28:13-15 (page _____ in the Old Testament): And there was the LORD standing beside him (Jacob). "I am the LORD, the God of Abraham and Isaac," He said. "I will give to you and to your descendants this land on which you are lying. They will be as numerous as the specks of dust on the earth. They will extend their territory in all directions, and through you and your descendants, I will bless all the nations. Remember, I will be with you and protect you wherever you go, and I will bring you back to this land. I will not leave you until I have done all that I have promised you."

2. **Jacob's name was changed to "Israel."**

   Genesis 35:9-15 (page _____ in the Old Testament): When Jacob returned from Mesopotamia, God appeared to him again and blessed him. God said to him, "Your name is Jacob, but from now on it will be Israel." So God named him Israel. And God said to him, "I am Almighty God. Have many children. Nations will be descended from you, and you will be the ancestor of kings. I will give you the land which I gave to Abraham and to Isaac, and I will also give it to your descendants after you."

God's Plan of Love

3. **Jacob's twelve sons became the leaders of the twelve tribes of Israel.**

   Genesis 49:1-2 (page _____ in the Old Testament): Jacob called for his sons and said, "Gather around, and I will tell you what will happen to you in the future: Come together and listen, sons of Jacob. Listen to your father Israel."

   Genesis 49: 28 (page _____ in the Old Testament): These are the twelve tribes of Israel, and this is what their Father said as he spoke a suitable word of farewell to each son.

4. **It was through the tribe of Judah, one of the twelve tribes, that God's Son came into the world.**

   Hebrews 7:13-14a (page _____ in the New Testament): And our LORD, of whom these things are said, belonged to a different tribe, and no member of His tribe ever served as a priest. It is well known that He was born a member of the tribe of Judah.

   > *John 3:16 (page _____ in the New Testament):* For God loved the world so much that He gave His only Son, so that everyone who believes in Him may not die but have eternal life.

Lesson 13

Joseph Chose God's Way

1. **God continued to carry out His plan through people.**

   Matthew 1:1-2a (page _____ in the New Testament): This is the list of the ancestors of Jesus Christ, a descendant of David, who was a descendant of Abraham. From Abraham to King David, the following ancestors are listed: Abraham, Isaac, Jacob, Judah and his brothers....

2. **Jacob and his twelve sons lived in the land of Canaan.**

   Genesis 37:1-2a (page _____ in the Old Testament): Jacob continued to live in the land of Canaan, where his father had lived, and this is the story of Jacob's family.

3. **Joseph was the best loved son.**

   Genesis 37:3 (page _____ in the Old Testament): Jacob loved Joseph more than all his other sons, because he had been born to him when he was old. He made a long robe with full sleeves for him.

4. **Joseph was hated by his brothers.**

   Genesis 37:4 (page _____ in the Old Testament): When his brothers saw that their father loved Joseph more than he loved them, they hated their brother so much that they would not speak to him in a friendly manner.

5. **Joseph was sold and taken to Egypt.**

   Genesis 37:28, 36 (page _____ in the Old Testament): And when some Midianite traders came by, the brothers pulled Joseph out of the well and sold him for twenty pieces of silver to the Ishmaelites, who took him to Egypt....Meanwhile, in Egypt the

Midianites had sold Joseph to Potiphar, one of the king's officers, who was the captain of the palace guard.

6. **God was with Joseph.**

   Genesis 39:2-3 (page _____ in the Old Testament): The LORD was with Joseph and made him successful. He lived in the house of his Egyptian master, who saw that the LORD was with Joseph and had made him successful in everything he did.

7. **Joseph was faithful to God.**

   Genesis 39:9b (page _____ in the Old Testament): How then could I do such an immoral thing and sin against God?

8. **Joseph was put in prison.**

   Genesis 39:19-20 (page _____ in the Old Testament): Joseph's master was furious and had Joseph arrested and put in the prison where the king's prisoners were kept, and there he stayed.

9. **God was with Joseph in prison.**

   Genesis 39:21 (page _____ in the Old Testament) and Acts 7: 9b-10a (page _____ in the New Testament): But the Lord was with Joseph and blessed him, so that the jailer was pleased with him. . . . But God was with him and brought him safely through all his troubles.

10. **Joseph was made a ruler in Egypt.**

    Genesis 41:38-41 (page _____ in the Old Testament) and Acts 7:10b (page _____ in the New Testament): And he said to them, "We will never find a better man than Joseph, a man who has God's spirit in him." The king said to Joseph, "God has shown you all this, so it is obvious that you have greater wisdom and insight than anyone else. I will put you in charge of my country, and all my people will obey your orders. Your authority will be second only to mine. I now appoint you governor over all Egypt. . . . When Joseph appeared before the king of Egypt, God gave him a pleasing manner and wisdom, and the king made Joseph governor over the country and royal household.

> **Romans 8:28 (page _____ in the New Testament): We know that in all things God works for good with those who love Him, those whom He has called according to His purpose.**

# Lesson 14

Joseph and His Brothers

1. **Pharaoh's dream came true just as Joseph had said it would.**

    Genesis 41:53-54 (page _____ in the Old Testament). The seven years of plenty that the land of Egypt had enjoyed came to an end, and the seven years of famine began, just as Joseph had said.

2. **Joseph's brothers went to Egypt to buy food.**

    Genesis 42:1-3 (page _____ in the Old Testament): When Jacob learned that there was grain in Egypt, he said to his sons, "Why don't you do something? I hear that there is grain in Egypt; go there and buy some to keep us from starving to death." So Joseph's ten half-brothers went to buy grain in Egypt.

3. **Joseph knew his brothers, but they did not know him.**

    Genesis 42:8 (page _____ in the Old Testament): Although Joseph recognized his brothers, they did not recognize him.

4. **Joseph's brothers began to feel sorry for what they had done to Joseph.**

    Genesis 42:21 (page _____ in the Old Testament): [They] said to one another, "Yes, now we are suffering the consequences of what we did to our brother; we saw the great trouble he was in when he begged for help, but we would not listen. That is why we are in this trouble now."

God's Plan of Love

5. **Joseph's brothers returned to Canaan.**

   Genesis 42:29 (page _____ in the Old Testament): When they came to their father Jacob in Canaan, they told him all that had happened to them.

6. **Joseph's brothers returned to Egypt with their brother, Benjamin.**

   Genesis 43:15a (page _____ in the Old Testament): So the brothers took the gifts and twice as much money, and set out for Egypt with Benjamin.

7. **Judah pled for Benjamin's life.**

   Genesis 44:33 (page _____ in the Old Testament): And now, sir, I will stay here as your slave in place of the boy; let him go back with his brothers.

8. **Joseph made himself known to his brothers.**

   Genesis 45:3-4 (page _____ in the Old Testament): Joseph said to his brothers, "I am Joseph. Is my father still alive?" But when his brothers heard this, they were so terrified that they could not answer. Then Joseph said to them, "Please come closer." They did, and he said, "I am your brother Joseph, whom you sold into Egypt."

9. **Joseph forgave his brothers.**

   Genesis 45:5, 7 (page _____ in the Old Testament): "Now do not be upset or blame yourselves because you sold me here. It was really God who sent me ahead of you to save people's lives....God sent me ahead of you to rescue you in this amazing way and to make sure that you and your descendants survive."

   > *1 John 1:9 (page _____ in the New Testament):* But if we confess our sins to God, He will keep His promise and do what is right; He will forgive us our sins and purify us from all our wrongdoing.

   > *Romans 8:28 (page _____ in the New Testament):* We know that in all things God works for good with those who love Him, those whom He has called according to His purpose.

Lesson 15

Joseph: A Part of God's Plan

1. **Joseph sent for his father, Jacob, to come to Egypt.**

   Genesis 45:9-10 (page _____ in the Old Testament): Now hurry back to my father and tell him that this is what his son Joseph says: "God has made me ruler of all Egypt; come to me without delay. You can live in the region of Goshen, where you can be near me—you, your children, your grandchildren, your sheep, your goats, your cattle, and everything else that you have."

2. **Jacob and his family went to Egypt.**

   Genesis 45:28 and Genesis 46:1 (page _____ in the Old Testament): "My son Joseph is still alive!" he said. "This is all I could ask for! I must go and see him before I die." Jacob packed up all he had and went to Beersheba, where he offered sacrifices to the God of his father Isaac.

3. **God comforted Jacob on his trip to Egypt.**

   Genesis 46:2-4 (page _____ in the Old Testament): God spoke to him in a vision at night and called, "Jacob, Jacob!" "Yes, here I am," he answered. "I am God, the God of your father," he said. "Do not be afraid to go to Egypt; I will make your descendants a great nation there. I will go with you to Egypt, and I will bring your descendants back to this land. Joseph will be with you when you die."

4. **Joseph went to Goshen to meet his father.**

   Genesis 46:29-30 (page _____ in the Old Testament): Joseph got in his chariot and went to Goshen to meet his father. When they met, Joseph threw his arms around his father's neck and cried for a long time. Jacob said to Joseph, "I am ready to die, now that I have seen you and know that you are still alive."

God's Plan of Love

5. **Jacob and all his family lived in the land of Egypt.**

   Genesis 47:11, 27 (page _____ in the Old Testament): Then Joseph settled his father and his brothers in Egypt, giving them property in the best of the land near the city of Rameses, as the king had commanded. . . . The Israelites lived in Egypt in the region of Goshen, where they became rich and had many children.

6. **Jacob died in Egypt. His body was taken back to Canaan.**

   Genesis 50:12-13 (page _____ in the Old Testament): So Jacob's sons did as he had commanded them; they carried his body to Canaan and buried it in the cave at Machpelah east of Mamre in the field which Abraham had bought from Ephron the Hittite for a burial ground.

7. **Joseph comforted his brothers.**

   Genesis 50:19-21 (page _____ in the Old Testament): But Joseph said to them, "Don't be afraid; I can't put myself in the place of God. You plotted evil against me, but God turned it into good, in order to preserve the lives of many people who are alive today because of what happened. You have nothing to fear. I will take care of you and your children." So he reassured them with kind words that touched their hearts.

8. **God continued to carry out His plan through Joseph.**

   Genesis 50:24 (page _____ in the Old Testament): He said to his brothers, "I am about to die, but God will certainly take care of you and lead you out of this land to the land he solemnly promised to Abraham, Isaac, and Jacob."

   > *John 3:16 (page _____ in the New Testament):* For God loved the world so much that He gave His only Son, so that everyone who believes in Him may not die but have eternal life.

   > *Romans 8:28 (page _____ in the New Testament):* We know that in all things God works for good with those who love Him, those whom He has called according to His purpose.

Part I: God's Plan through the Bible

Lesson 16

God's People in Egypt

1. **God continued to carry out His plan for His people.**

   Exodus 1:6:7 (page _____ in the Old Testament): In the course of time Joseph, his brothers, and all the rest of that generation died, but their descendants, the Israelites, had many children and became so numerous and strong that Egypt was filled with them.

2. **A new king ruled Egypt.**

   Exodus 1:8 (page _____ in the Old Testament): Then, a new king, who knew nothing about Joseph, came to power in Egypt.

3. **The Egyptians made slaves of the Israelites.**

   Exodus 1:12b-14 (page _____ in the Old Testament): The Egyptians came to fear the Israelites and made their lives miserable by forcing them into cruel slavery. They made them work on their building projects and in their fields, and they had no pity on them.

4. **The king ordered all Israelite (Hebrew) baby boys to be killed.**

   Exodus 1:22 (page _____ in the Old Testament): Finally the king issued a command to all his people: "Take every newborn Hebrew boy and throw him into the Nile, but let all the girls live."

5. **Baby boy Moses was born into an Israelite (Hebrew) family.**

    Exodus 2:1-2a (page _____ in the Old Testament): During this time a man from the tribe of Levi married a woman of his own tribe, and she bore him a son.

6. **The family had a plan to save their baby boy, Moses.**

    Exodus 2:3-4 (page _____ in the Old Testament): But when she could not hide him any longer, she took a basket made of reeds and covered it with tar to make it watertight. She put the baby in it and then replaced it in the tall grass at the edge of the river.

    Hebrews 11:23 (page _____ in the New Testament): It was faith that made the parents of Moses hide him for three months after he was born. They saw that he was a beautiful child, and they were not afraid to disobey the king's order.

7. **The king's daughter found Moses and saved his life.**

    Exodus 2:5, 9-10 (page _____ in the Old Testament): The king's daughter came down to the river to bathe, while her servants walked along the bank. Suddenly she noticed the basket in the tall grass and sent a slave girl to get it. . . . The princess told the woman, "Take this baby and nurse him for me, and I will pay you." So she took the baby and nursed him. Later, when the child was old enough, she took him to the king's daughter, who adopted him as her own son. She said to herself, "I pulled him out of the water, and so I name him Moses."

8. **Moses grew up in the king's palace.**

    Exodus 2:11a (page _____ in the Old Testament): When Moses had grown up. . . .

    Acts 7:21b-22 (page _____ in the New Testament): …the king's daughter adopted him and brought him up as her own son. He was taught all the wisdom of the Egyptians and became a great man in words and deeds.

9. **Moses visited his father's people, the Israelites (Hebrews).**

   Exodus 2:11b (page _____ in the Old Testament): He went out to visit his people.

   Acts 7:23 (page _____ in the New Testament): When Moses was forty years old, he decided to find out how his fellow Israelites were being treated.

10. **Moses killed an Egyptian.**

    Exodus 2:11c-12 (page _____ in the Old Testament): And he saw how they were forced to do hard labor. He even saw an Egyptian kill a Hebrew, one of Moses' own people. Moses looked all around, and when he saw that no one was watching, he killed the Egyptian and hid his body in the sand.

    Acts 7:24 (page _____ in the New Testament): He saw one of them being mistreated by an Egyptian, so he went to his help and took revenge on the Egyptian by killing him.

11. **Moses went to the land of Midian to live.**

    Exodus 2:15-16 (page _____ in the Old Testament): When the king heard about what had happened, he tried to have Moses killed, but Moses fled and went to live in the land of Midian.

12. **God cared for His people in Egypt.**

    Exodus 2:23-25 (page _____ in the Old Testament): Years later the king of Egypt died, but the Israelites were still groaning under their slavery and cried out for help. Their cry went up to God, who heard their groaning and remembered his covenant with Abraham, Isaac, and Jacob. He saw the slavery of the Israelites and was concerned for them.

13. **God cares for EVERYONE!**

    John 3:16 (page _____ in the New Testament): For God loved the world so much that He gave His only Son, so that everyone who believes in Him may not die but have eternal life.

God's Plan of Love

Fill the blank spaces in the sentences below with one of these words:

eternal life   Hebrew   boy   miserable   slavery

children   river   Egyptian   only   Son   three

Moses   faith   deeds   Egypt   basket   words

Midian   everyone   who

1. The Israelites had many _____ and became so numerous and strong that _____ was filled with them.

2. The Egyptians came to fear the Israelites and made their lives _____ by forcing them into cruel _____.

3. The king said, "Take every newborn _____ _____ and throw him in the Nile."

4. When the family could no longer hide baby Moses, they put him in a _____ and placed it in the _____.

5. It was _____ that made the parents of Moses hide him for _____ months.

6. The princess said, "I pulled him out of the water; I will name him _____."

7. Moses became a great man in _____ and _____.

8. Moses saw an Egyptian kill a Hebrew, so he took revenge by killing an _____.

9. Moses went to live in the land of _____.

10. God loved the world so much that He gave His _____ _____ so that _____ _____ believes in Him shall have _____ _____!

Lesson 17

God Called Moses

1. **Moses saw a burning bush at Mt. Sinai.**

   Exodus 3:2 (page _____ in the Old Testament): There the angel of the LORD appeared to him as a flame coming from the middle of a bush. Moses saw that the bush was on fire but that it was not burning up.

2. **God spoke to Moses from the burning bush.**

   Exodus 3:4-6 (page _____ in the Old Testament): When the LORD saw that Moses was coming closer, He called to him from the middle of the bush and said, "Moses! Moses!" He answered, "Yes, here I am." God said, "Do not come any closer. Take off your sandals, because you are standing on holy ground. I am the God of your ancestors, the God of Abraham, Isaac, and Jacob." So Moses covered his face, because he was afraid to look at God.

3. **God told Moses to lead His people out of Egypt.**

   Exodus 3:10 (page _____ in the Old Testament): Now I am sending you to the king of Egypt so that you can lead My people out of his country.

God's Plan of Love

4. Moses gave excuses. God gave promises.

Moses' Excuses	God's Promises
"I am nobody." *Exodus 3:11 (page _____ in the Old Testament): But Moses said to God, "I am nobody. How can I go to the king and bring the Israelites out of Egypt?"*	"I will be with you." *Exodus 3:12 (page _____ in the Old Testament): God answered, "I will be with you, and when you bring the people out of Egypt, you will worship Me on this mountain. That will be the proof that I have sent you."*
"I don't know your name." *Exodus 3:13 (page _____ in the Old Testament): But Moses replied, "When I go to the Israelites and say to them, 'The God of your ancestors sent me to you,' they will ask me, 'What is His name?' So what can I tell them?"*	"My name is I AM." *Exodus 3:14-15 (page _____ in the Old Testament): God said, "I am who I am. You must tell them: 'The One who is called I AM has sent me to you.' Tell the Israelites that I, the LORD, the God of your ancestors, the God of Abraham, Isaac, and Jacob, have sent you to them. This is My name forever; this is what all future generations are to call Me."*
"The Israelites may not believe me." *Exodus 4:1 (page _____ in the Old Testament): Then Moses answered the LORD, "But suppose the Israelites do not believe me and will not listen to what I say. What shall I do if they say that You did not appear to me?"*	"You will show My miracles." *Exodus 4:5 (page _____ in the Old Testament): The LORD said, "Do this to prove to the Israelites that the LORD, the God of their ancestors, and God of Abraham, Isaac, and Jacob, has appeared to you."*
"I am not a good speaker." *Exodus 4:10 (page _____ in the Old Testament): But Moses said, "No, LORD, don't send me. I have never been a good speaker, and I haven't become one since You began to speak to me. I am a poor speaker, slow and hesitant."*	"I will tell you what to say." *Exodus 4:12 (page _____ in the Old Testament): "Now, go! I will help you to speak, and I will tell you what to say."*

Part I: God's Plan through the Bible

"Let somebody else go." *Exodus 4:13 (page _____ in the Old Testament):* But Moses answered, "No, LORD, please send someone else."	"I will help you." *Exodus 4:15b, 17 (page _____ in the Old Testament):* "I will help both of you to speak, and I will tell you both what to do. . . . Take this walking stick with you; for with it you will perform miracles."

5. God helps EVERYONE today.

Philippians 4:19-20 (page _____ in the New Testament): And with all His abundant wealth through Christ Jesus, my God will supply all your needs. To our God and Father be the glory forever and ever! Amen.

Read Moses' excuses given below. Also read God's promises. Then write the correct letter of God's promise on the line next to Moses' excuse.

MOSES' EXCUSES:

_____ 1. "I am not a good speaker."

_____ 2. "I am a nobody."

_____ 3. "Let somebody else go."

_____ 4. "The Israelites may not believe me."

_____ 5. "I don't know your name."

GOD'S PROMISES:

a. "I will help you."

b. "You will show My miracles."

c. "My name is I AM."

d. "I will tell you what to say."

e. "I will be with you."

Lesson 18

God's Plan for Moses

1. **God promised Moses that his brother, Aaron, would help him.**

   Exodus 4:14-15 (page _____ in the Old Testament): At this the LORD became angry with Moses and said, "What about your brother Aaron, the Levite? I know that he can speak well. In fact, he is now coming to meet you and will be glad to see you. You can speak to him and tell him what to say. I will help both of you to speak, and I will tell you both what to do."

2. **Moses and Aaron went to Egypt.**

   Exodus 4:29 (page _____ in the Old Testament): So Moses and Aaron gathered all the Israelite leaders together.

3. **The Israelites believed Moses and Aaron.**

   Exodus 4:30-31 (page _____ in the Old Testament): Aaron told them everything that the LORD had said to Moses and then Moses performed all the miracles in front of the people. They believed, and when they heard that the LORD had come to them and had seen how they were being treated cruelly, they bowed down and worshiped.

4. **Moses and Aaron went to see the king of Egypt.**

   Exodus 5:1-2 (page _____ in the Old Testament): Then Moses and Aaron went to the king of Egypt and said, "The LORD, the God of Israel, says, 'Let My people go, so that they can hold a festival in the desert to honor Me.'" "Who is the LORD?" the king demanded. "Why should I listen to Him and let Israel go? I do not know the LORD; and I will not let Israel go."

5. **The king would not let the Israelites go.**

    Exodus 5:2b (page _____ in the Old Testament): Why should I listen to him and let Israel go? I do not know the LORD; and I will not let Israel go.

6. **The king gave the Israelites very hard work to do.**

    Exodus 5:4, 10-11 (page _____ in the Old Testament): The king said to Moses and Aaron, "What do you mean by making the people neglect their work? Get those slaves back to work!" . . . The slave drivers and the Israelite foremen went out and said to the Israelites, "The king has said that he will not supply you with any more straw. He says that you must go and get it for yourselves wherever you can find it, but you must still make the same number of bricks."

7. **God gave His promise to the Israelites again.**

    Exodus 6:4 (page _____ in the Old Testament): I also made My covenant with them, promising to give them the land of Canaan, the land in which they had lived as foreigners.

    Exodus 6:6-8 (page _____ in the Old Testament): So tell the Israelites that I say to them, "I am the LORD; I will rescue you and set you free from your slavery to the Egyptians. I will raise My mighty arm to bring terrible punishment upon them, and I will save you. I will make you My own people, and I will be your God. You will know that I am the LORD your God when I set you free from slavery in Egypt. I will bring you to the land that I solemnly promised to give to Abraham, Isaac, and Jacob; and I will give it to you as your own possession. I am the LORD."

8. **God gave a picture of His plan for us.**

    John 3:16 (page _____ in the New Testament): For God loved the world so much that He gave His only Son, so that everyone who believes in Him may not die but have eternal life.

God's Plan of Love

God's Picture	God's Promises
"I will rescue you and set you free."	*Galatians 5.1a (page _____ in the New Testament): "Freedom is what we have—Christ has set us free!"*
"I will save you."	*Matthew 1:21 (page _____ in the New Testament): "She will have a Son, and you will name Him JESUS—because He will save His people from their sins."*
"I will make you My own people."	*1 Peter 2:9 (page _____ in the New Testament): "But you are the chosen race, the King's priests, the holy nation, God's own people, chosen to proclaim the wonderful acts of God, who called you out of darkness into His own marvelous light."*
"I will be your God."	*Hebrews 8:10 (page _____ in the New Testament): "Now, this is a covenant that I will make with the people of Israel in the days to come, says the LORD: I will put My laws in their minds and write them on their hearts. I will be their God, and they will be My people."*
"I will bring you to the land I promised."	*Hebrews 4:3a (page _____ in the New Testament): "We who believe, then, do receive that rest which God promised."*

9. **God's plan for us today is the same as it was in the days of Moses!**

   Hebrews 13:8 (page _____ in the New Testament): Jesus Christ is the same yesterday, today, and forever!

Lesson 19

God's Plan to Free the Israelites

God made man like Himself.

Genesis 1:27a (page _____ in the Old Testament): So God created human beings, making them to be like Himself.

God made man free to choose.

Genesis 2:16-17 (page _____ in the Old Testament): He told him, "You may eat the fruit of any tree in the garden, except the tree that gives knowledge of what is good and what is bad. You must not eat the fruit of that tree; if you do, you will die the same day."

Man chose his own way.

Genesis 3:6 (page _____ in the Old Testament): The woman saw how beautiful the tree was and how good its fruit would be to eat, and she thought how wonderful it would be to become wise. So she took some of the fruit and ate it. Then she gave some to her husband, and he also ate it.

Sin is choosing my own way.

Isaiah 53:6 (page _____ in the Old Testament): All of us were like sheep that were lost, each of us going his own way. But the LORD made the punishment fall on Him, the punishment all of us deserved.

Abraham chose God's way.

Genesis 12:4 (page _____ in the Old Testament): When Abram was seventy-five years old, he started out from Haran, as the LORD had told him to do; and Lot went with him.

Joseph chose God's way.

Acts 7:9b, 10a (page _____ in the New Testament): But God was with him and brought him safely through all his troubles.

God's Plan of Love

Moses chose God's way.

Exodus 4:29 (page _____ in the Old Testament): So Moses and Aaron went to Egypt and gathered all the Israelite leaders together.

1. **The Lord told Moses and Aaron to speak to the king.**

    Exodus 6:13 (page _____ in the Old Testament): The LORD commanded Moses and Aaron: "Tell the Israelites and the king of Egypt that I have ordered you to lead the Israelites out of Egypt."

2. **The king would not listen.**

    Exodus 7:13 (page _____ in the Old Testament): The king, however, remained stubborn and, just as the LORD had said, the king would not listen to Moses and Aaron.

3. **God sent disasters to the Egyptians.**

    i. Blood—Exodus 7:14-25 (page _____ in the Old Testament)

    ii. Frogs—Exodus 8:1-15 (page _____ in the Old Testament)

    iii. Gnats—Exodus 8:16-19 (page _____ in the Old Testament)

    iv. Flies—Exodus 8:20-32 (page _____ in the Old Testament)

    v. Death of animals—Exodus 9:1-7 (page _____ in the Old Testament)

    vi. Boils—Exodus 9:8-12 (page _____ in the Old Testament)

    vii. Hail—Exodus 8:13-35 (page _____ in the Old Testament)

    viii. Locusts—Exodus 10:1-20 (page _____ in the Old Testament)

    ix. Darkness—Exodus 10:21-26 (page _____ in the Old Testament)

4. **The king continued to say, "NO!"**

    Exodus 10:27 (page _____ in the Old Testament): The LORD made the king stubborn, and he would not let them go.

5. **God sent the worst disaster to the Egyptians.**

    Exodus 11:4-5 (page _____ in the Old Testament): Moses then said to the king, "The LORD says, 'At about midnight, I will go through Egypt, and every first-born son in Egypt will die, from the king's son, who is heir to the throne, to the son of the slave woman who grinds grain. The firstborn of all the cattle will die also.'"

Part I: God's Plan through the Bible

6. **God had a plan to save the Israelites.**

    Exodus 12:12-13 (page _____ in the Old Testament): "On that night I will go through the land of Egypt, killing every firstborn male, both human and animal, and punishing all the gods of Egypt. I am the LORD. The blood on the doorposts will be a sign to mark the houses in which you live. When I see the blood, I will pass over you and will not harm you when I punish the Egyptians."

God's Plan for the Israelites in Egypt	God's Plan for Everyone Today
Choose a perfect sheep. *Exodus 12:5 (page _____ in the Old Testament): "You may choose either a sheep or a goat, but it must be a one-year-old male without any defects."*	*John 1:29 (page _____ in the New Testament): The next day John saw Jesus coming to him, and said, "There is the Lamb of God, who takes away the sin of the world!"*
Kill the sheep. *Exodus 12:6 (page _____ in the Old Testament): Then, on the evening of the fourteenth day of the month, the whole community of Israel will kill the animals.*	*Hebrews 9:28a (page _____ in the New Testament): In the same manner Christ also was offered in sacrifice once to take away the sins of many.*
Put the blood on the doorposts. *Exodus 12:22 (page _____ in the Old Testament): Take a sprig of hyssop, dip it in the bowl containing the animal's blood, and wipe the blood on the doorposts and the beam above the door of your house. Not one of you is to leave the house until morning.*	*Hebrews 9:12 (page _____ in the New Testament): When Christ went through the tent and entered once and for all into the Most Holy Place, He did not take the blood of goats and bulls to offer as a sacrifice; rather, He took His own blood and obtained eternal salvation for us.*

7. **The Israelites chose God's plan.**

    Exodus 12:27b-28 (page _____ in the Old Testament): The Israelites knelt down and worshiped. Then they went and did what the LORD had commanded Moses and Aaron.

8. **Today EVERYONE must choose.**

    John 3:16 (page _____ in the New Testament): For God loved the world so much that He gave His only Son, so that EVERYONE who believes in Him may not die, but have eternal life.

Lesson 20

The Israelites Chose God's Plan

1. **God had a plan to save the Israelites.**

    Exodus 12:12-13 (page _____ in the Old Testament): "On that night I will go through the land of Egypt, killing every firstborn male, both human and animal, and punishing all the gods of Egypt. I am the LORD. The blood on the doorposts will be a sign to mark the houses in which you live. When I see the blood, I will pass over you and will not harm you when I punish the Egyptians."

2. **The Israelites chose God's plan.**

    Exodus 12:28 (page _____ in the Old Testament): Then they went and did what the LORD had commanded Moses and Aaron.

3. **The Israelites left Egypt.**

    Exodus 12:37a, 40-42 (page _____ in the Old Testament): The Israelites set out on foot from Rameses for Sukkoth....The Israelites had lived in Egypt for 430 years. On the day the 430 years ended, all the tribes of the LORD'S people left Egypt. It was a night when the LORD kept watch to bring them out of Egypt; this same night is dedicated to the LORD for all time to come as a night when the Israelites must keep watch.

4. **God led the Israelites with cloud and fire.**

    Exodus 13:20-21 (page _____ in the Old Testament): The Israelites left Sukkoth and camped at Etham on the edge of the desert. During the day the LORD went in front of them in a pillar of cloud to show them the way, and during the night He went in front of them in a pillar of fire to give them light, so that they could travel night and day.

5. **The Egyptians chased the Israelites.**

    Exodus 14:5-7 (page _____ in the Old Testament): When the king of Egypt was told that the people had escaped, he and his officials changed their minds and said, "What have we done? We have let the Israelites escape, and we have lost them as our slaves!" The king got his war chariot and his army ready. He set out with all his chariots, including the six hundred finest, commanded by their officers.

6. **The Israelites were afraid of the Egyptians.**

    Exodus 14:10 (page _____ in the Old Testament): When the Israelites saw the king and his army marching against them, they were terrified and cried out to the LORD for help.

Part I: God's Plan through the Bible

7. **Moses told the Israelites not to be afraid.**

    Exodus 14:13-14 (page _____ in the Old Testament): Moses answered, "Don't be afraid! Stand your ground, and you will see what the LORD will do to save you today; you will never see these Egyptians again. The LORD will fight for you, and all you have to do is keep still."

8. **God took the Israelites safely through the Red Sea.**

    Exodus 14:21-22 (page _____ in the Old Testament): Moses held out his hand over the sea, and the LORD drove the sea back with a strong east wind. It blew all night and turned the sea into dry land. The water was divided, and the Israelites went through the sea on dry ground, with walls of water on both sides.

9. **God destroyed the Egyptians in the Red Sea.**

    Exodus 14:27b-28 (page _____ in the Old Testament): The Egyptians tried to escape from the water, but the LORD threw them into the sea. The water returned and covered the chariots, the drivers, and all the Egyptian army that had followed the Israelites into the sea; not one of them was left.

10. **The Israelites complained many times.**

    i. Bitter water

    Exodus 15:22-27 (page _____ in the Old Testament): Then Moses led the people of Israel away from the Red Sea into the desert of Shur. For three days they walked through the desert, but found no water. Then they came to a place called Marah, but the water there was so bitter that they could not drink it. That is why it was named Marah. The people complained to Moses and asked, "What are we going to drink?" Moses prayed earnestly to the LORD, and the LORD showed him a piece of wood, which he threw into the water; and the water became fit to drink. There the LORD gave them laws to live by, and there He also tested them. He said, "If you will obey Me completely by doing what I consider right and by keeping My commands, I will not punish you with any of the diseases that I brought on the Egyptians. I am the LORD, the One who heals you." Next they came to Elim, where there were twelve springs and seventy palm trees; there they camped by the water.

    ii. No food

    Exodus 16:1-36 (page _____ in the Old Testament): The whole Israelite community set out from Elim, and on the fifteenth day of the second month after they had left Egypt, they came to the desert of Sin, which is between Elim and Sinai. There in the desert they all complained to Moses and Aaron and said to them, "We wish that the LORD had killed us in Egypt. There we could at least sit down and eat meat and as much other food as we wanted. But you have brought us out into this desert to starve us all to death." The LORD said to Moses, "Now I am going to cause food to rain down from the sky for all of you. The people must go out every day and gather enough for that day. In this way I can test them to find out if they will follow My instructions. . . . On the sixth day they are to bring in twice as much as usual and prepare it." So Moses and Aaron said to all the Israelites, "This evening you will know that it was the LORD who brought you out of Egypt. In the morning you will see the dazzling light of the LORD'S presence. He has heard your complaints against Him-yes, against Him, because we are only carrying out His instructions." Then Moses said, "It is the LORD who will give you meat to eat in the evening and as much bread as you want in the morning, because He has heard how much you have complained against Him. When you complain against us, you are really complaining against the LORD." Moses said to Aaron, 'Tell the whole community to come and stand before the LORD, because He has heard their complaints." As Aaron spoke to the whole community, they turned toward the desert, and suddenly the dazzling light of the LORD appeared in a cloud. The LORD said to Moses, "I have heard the complaints of the Israelites. Tell them that at twilight they will have meat to eat, and in the morning they will have all the bread they want. Then they will know that I, the LORD, am their God." In the evening a large flock of quails flew in, enough to cover the camp, and in the morning there was dew all around the camp. When the dew evaporated, there was something thin and flaky on the surface of the desert. It was as delicate as frost. When the Israelites saw it, they didn't know what it was and asked each other, "What is it?" Moses said to them, 'This is the food that the LORD has given you to eat. The LORD has commanded that each of you is to gather as much of it as he needs, two quarts for each member of his household." The Israelites did this, some gathering more, others less. When they measured it, those who gathered much did not have too much, and those who gathered less did not have too little. Each had gathered just what he needed. Moses said to them, "No one is to keep any of it for tomorrow." But some of them did not listen to Moses and saved part of it. The next morning it was full of worms and smelled rotten, and Moses was angry with them. Every morning each one gathered as much as he needed; and when the sun grew hot, what was left on the ground melted. On the sixth day they gathered twice as much food, four quarts for each person. All the leaders of the community came and told Moses about it, and he said to them, "The LORD has commanded that tomorrow is a holy day of rest, dedicated to Him. Bake today what you want to bake and boil what you want to boil. Whatever is left should be put aside and kept for tomorrow." As Moses had commanded, they kept what was left until the next day; it did not spoil or get worms in it. Moses said, "Eat this today, because today is the Sabbath, a day of rest dedicated to the LORD, and you will not find any food outside the camp. You must gather food for six days, but on the seventh day, the day of rest, there will be none. "On the seventh day some of the people went out to gather food, but they did not find any. Then the LORD said to Moses, "How much longer will you people refuse to obey My commands? Remember that I, the LORD, have given you a day of rest, and that is why on the sixth day I will always give you enough food for two days. Everyone is to stay where he is on the seventh day and not leave his home." So the people did no work on the seventh day. The people of Israel called the food manna. It was like a small white seed, and tasted like thin cakes, made with honey. Moses said, "The LORD has commanded us to save some manna to be kept for our descendants, so that they can see the food which He gave us to eat in the desert when He brought us out of

Egypt." Moses said to Aaron, "Take a jar, put two quarts of manna in it and place it in the LORD's presence to be kept for our descendants." As the LORD had commanded Moses, Aaron put it in front of the Covenant Box, so that it could be kept. The Israelites ate manna for the next forty years, until they reached the land of Canaan, where they settled. (The standard dry measure then in use equaled twenty quarts.)

    iii. No water

Exodus 17:1-7 (page _____ in the Old Testament): The whole Israelite community left the desert of Sin, moving from one place to another at the command of the LORD. They camped at Rephidim, but there was no water there to drink. They complained to Moses and said, "Give us water to drink." Moses answered, "Why are you complaining? Why are you putting the LORD to the test?" But the people were very thirsty and continued to complain to Moses. They said, "Why did you bring us out of Egypt? To kill us and our children and our livestock with thirst?" Moses prayed earnestly to the LORD and said, "What can I do with these people? They are almost ready to stone me." The LORD said to Moses, "Take some of the leaders of Israel with you, and go on ahead of the people. Take along the stick with which you struck the Nile. I will stand before you on a rock at Mount Sinai. Strike the rock, and water will come out of it for the people to drink." Moses did so in the presence of the leaders of Israel. The place was named Massah and Meribah, because the Israelites complained and put the LORD to the test when they asked, "Is the LORD with us or not?"

11. The Israelites went to Mount Sinai.

Exodus 19:1-2 (page _____ in the Old Testament): The people of Israel left Rephidim, and on the first day of the third month after they had left Egypt they came to the desert of Sinai. There they set up camp at the foot of Mount Sinai.

12. God sets us free today.

Ephesians 1:6-7 (page _____ in the New Testament): Let us praise God for His glorious grace, for the free gift he gave us in His dear Son! For by the sacrificial death of Christ we are set free, that is, our sins are forgiven. How great is the grace of God!

Read number 12 above and write in the missing words in the Bible verse below.

Let us _____ God for His glorious _____, for the _____ gift He gave us in His dear _____! For by the _____ _____ of _____ we are set _____, that is, our _____ are _____. How great is the _____ of God!

Lesson 21

God Gave the Ten Commandments

1. **Moses told the Israelites not to be afraid.**

   Exodus 14:13-14 (page _____ in the Old Testament): Moses answered, "Don't be afraid! Stand your ground, and you will see what the LORD will do to save you today; you will never see these Egyptians again. The LORD will fight for you, and all you have to do is keep still."

2. **God took the Israelites safely through the Red Sea.**

   Exodus 14:21-22 (page _____ in the Old Testament): Moses held out his hand over the sea, and the LORD drove the sea back with a strong east wind. It blew all night and turned the sea into dry land. The water was divided, and the Israelites went through the sea on dry ground, with walls of water on both sides.

3. **God destroyed the Egyptians in the Red Sea.**

   Exodus 14:27b-28 (page _____ in the Old Testament): The Egyptians tried to escape from the water, but the LORD threw them into the sea. The water returned and covered the chariots, the drivers, and all the Egyptian army that had followed the Israelites into the sea; not one of them was left.

4. **The Israelites had faith in the Lord and in His servant, Moses.**

   Exodus 14:31 (page _____ in the Old Testament): When the Israelites saw the great power with which the LORD had defeated the Egyptians, they stood in awe of the LORD; and they had faith in the LORD and in His servant Moses.

5. **The Israelites complained many times.**
   i. Bitter water—*Exodus 15:22-27 (page _____ in the Old Testament).* See Lesson 20.

Part I: God's Plan through the Bible

ii. No food—Exodus 16:1-36 (page _____ in the Old Testament). See Lesson 20

iii. No water—Exodus 17:1-7 (page _____ in the Old Testament). See Lesson 20.

6. The Israelites camped at Mount Sinai.

Exodus 19:1-2 (page _____ in the Old Testament): The people of Israel left Rephidim, and on the first day of the third month after they had left Egypt, they came to the desert of Sinai. There they set up camp at the foot of Mount Sinai.

7. Moses went up Mount Sinai to meet God.

Exodus 19:3 (page _____ in the Old Testament): And Moses went up on the mountain to meet with God.

8. God spoke laws (commandments) for the Israelites.

Exodus 20:1-17 (page _____ in the Old Testament): God spoke and these were His words: "I am the LORD your God who brought you out of Egypt, where you were slaves.

"Worship no god but Me.

"Do not make for yourselves images of anything in heaven or on earth or in the water under the earth.

"Do not bow down to any idol or worship it, because I am the LORD your God and I tolerate no rivals. I bring punishment on those who hate Me and on their descendants down to the third and found generation. But I show My love to thousands of generations of those who love Me and obey My laws.

"Do not use My name for evil purposes, for I, the LORD your God, will punish anyone who misuses My name.

"Observe the Sabbath and keep it holy. You have six days in which to do your work, but the seventh day is a day of rest dedicated to Me. On that day no one is to work—neither you, your children, your slaves, your animals, nor the foreigners who live in your country. In six days I, the LORD, made the earth, the sky, the seas, and everything in them, but on the seventh day I rested. That is why I, the LORD, blessed the Sabbath and made it holy.

"Respect your father and your mother, so that you may live a long time in the land that I am giving you.

"Do not commit murder.

"Do not commit adultery.

"Do not steal.

"Do not accuse anyone falsely.

"Do not desire another man's house; do not desire his wife, his slaves, his cattle, his donkeys, or anything that he owns."

God's Plan of Love

i. The laws (commandments) were given after God had saved the Israelites.

Exodus 20:2 (page _____ in the Old Testament): "I am the LORD your God who brought you out of Egypt, where you were slaves."

ii. The laws (commandments) were given to the Israelites to show them how to live as God's chosen people.

Exodus 20:20 (page _____ in the Old Testament): Moses replied, "Don't be afraid; God has only come to test you and make you keep on obeying Him, so that you will not sin."

1 Peter 2:9 (page _____ in the New Testament): But you are the chosen race, the King's priests, the holy nation, God's own people, chosen to proclaim the wonderful acts of God, who called you out of darkness into His own marvelous light.

iii. The laws (commandments), one through four, showed the Israelites how they should feel (act) toward God.

Exodus 20:3-11 (page _____ in the Old Testament): "Worship no god but Me. Do not make for yourselves images of anything in heaven or on earth or in the water under the earth. Do not bow down to any idol or worship it, because I am the LORD your God and I tolerate no rivals. I bring punishment on those who hate Me and on their descendants down to the third and fourth generation. But I show My love to thousands of generations of those who love Me and obey My laws. Do not use My name for evil purposes, for I, the LORD your God, will punish anyone who misuses My name. Observe the Sabbath and keep it holy. You have six days in which to do your work, but the seventh day is a day of rest dedicated to Me. On that day no one is to work—neither you, your children, your slaves, your animals, nor the foreigners who live in your country. In six days I, the LORD, made the earth, the sky, the seas, and everything in them, but on the seventh day I rested. That is why I, the LORD, blessed the Sabbath and made it holy."

iv. The laws (commandments), five through ten, showed the Israelites how they should feel (act) toward other people.

Exodus 20:12-17 (page _____ in the Old Testament): "Respect your father and mother, so that you may live a long time in the land that I am giving you. Do not commit murder. Do not commit adultery. Do not steal. Do not accuse anyone falsely. Do not desire another man's house; do not desire his wife, his slaves, his cattle, his donkeys, or anything else that he owns."

9. Jesus told about the laws (commandments).

Mark 12:29-33 (page _____ in the New Testament): Jesus replied, "The most important one is this: 'Listen, Israel! The LORD our God is the only LORD. Love the LORD your God with all your heart, with all your soul, with all your mind, and with all your strength.' The second most important commandment is this: 'Love your neighbor as you love yourself.' There is no other commandment more important that these two." The teacher of the Law said to Jesus, "Well done, Teacher! It is true, as You say, that only the LORD is God and that there is no other god but He. And man must love God with all his heart and with all his mind and with all his strength; and he must love his neighbor as he loves himself. It is more important to obey these two commandments than to offer on the altar animals and other sacrifices to God."

Lesson 22

The Journey to the Promised Land

1. **God spoke laws (commandments) to the Israelites:**

    i. To show them how to live as God's chosen people.

    Exodus 20:20 (page _____ in the Old Testament): Moses replied, "Don't be afraid; God has only come to test you and make you keep on obeying Him, so that you will not sin."

    ii. To show them how they should feel (act) toward God.

    Exodus 20:3-11 (page _____ in the Old Testament): #1: "Worship no god but Me." #2: "Do not make for yourselves images of anything in heaven or on earth or in the water under the earth." #3: "Do not use My name for evil purposes." #4: "Observe the Sabbath and keep it holy."

    iii. To show them how they should feel (act) toward other people.

    Exodus 20:12-17 (page _____ in the Old Testament): #5: "Respect your father and your mother." #6: "Do not commit murder." #7: "Do not commit adultery." #8: "Do not steal." #9: "Do not accuse anyone falsely." #10: "Do not desire another man's house, do not desire his wife, his slaves, his cattle, his donkeys, or anything else that he owns."

2. **Moses told the people all of the Lord's laws (commandments). The people chose to obey.**

    Exodus 24:3 (page _____ in the Old Testament): Moses went and told the people all the LORD's commands and all the ordinances, and all the people answered together, "We will do everything that the LORD has said."

3. **God gave the people His plan for them to build a Tent for worship.**

    Exodus 25:8-9 (page _____ in the Old Testament): "The people must make a sacred Tent for Me, so that I may live among them. Make it and all its furnishings according to the plan that I will show you."

God's Plan of Love

4. **God showed His presence at the Tent of worship.**

   Exodus 33:9-10 (page _____ in the Old Testament): After Moses had gone in, the pillar of cloud would come down and stay at the door of the Tent, and the LORD would speak to Moses from the cloud. As soon as the people saw the pillar of cloud at the door of the Tent, they would bow down.

5. **The book of Leviticus told the people God's laws (commandments) about worship, offerings, and sacrifices.**

   Leviticus 27:34 (page _____ in the Old Testament): These are the commands that the LORD gave Moses on Mount Sinai for the people of Israel.

   i. Offerings were made as an act of thanksgiving.

   ii. Sacrifices were made as a confession of sins.

6. **The Israelites left Mount Sinai.**

   Numbers 10:11-12 (page _____ in the Old Testament): On the twentieth day of the second month in the second year after the people left Egypt, the cloud over the Tent of the LORD's presence lifted, and the Israelites started on their journey out of the Sinai Desert. The cloud came to rest in the wilderness of Paran.

7. **The Israelites continued to complain.**

   Numbers 20:5 (page _____ in the Old Testament): "Why did you bring us out of Egypt into this miserable place where nothing will grow? There's no grain, no figs, no grapes, no pomegranates. There is not even any water to drink!"

8. **Moses disobeyed God.**

   Numbers 20:7-12 (page _____ in the Old Testament): The LORD said to Moses, "Take the stick that is in front of the Covenant Box, and then you and Aaron assemble the whole community. There in front of them all speak to that rock over there, and water will gush out of it. In this way you will bring water out of the rock for the people, for them and their animals to drink." Moses went and got the stick, as the LORD had commanded, he and Aaron assembled the whole community in front of the rock, and Moses said, "Listen, you rebels! Do we have to get water out of this rock for you?" Then Moses raised the stick and struck the rock twice with it, and a great stream of water gushed out, and all the people and animals drank. But the LORD reprimanded Moses and Aaron. He said, "Because you did not have enough faith to acknowledge My holy power before the people of Israel, you will not lead them into the land that I promised to give them."

9. **Joshua was chosen to succeed Moses.**

   Deuteronomy 31:1-3, 6-8 (page _____ in the Old Testament): Moses continued speaking to the people of Israel, and said, "I am now a hundred and twenty years old and am no longer able to be your leader. And besides this, the LORD has told me that I will not cross the Jordan. The LORD your God Himself will go before you and destroy the nations living there, so that you can occupy their land; and Joshua will be your leader, as the LORD has said....Be determined and confident. Do not be afraid of them. Your God, the LORD Himself, will be with you. He will not fail you or abandon you." Then Moses called Joshua and said to him in the presence of all the people of Israel, "Be determined and confident; you are the one who will lead these people to occupy the land that the LORD promised to their ancestors. The LORD Himself will lead you and be with you. He will not fail you or abandon you, so do not lose courage or be afraid."

The LORD showed him the whole land.

10. God showed Moses the Promised Land.

Deuteronomy 34:1a, 4 (page _____ in the Old Testament): Moses went up from the plains of Moab to Mount Nebo, to the top of Mount Pisgah east of Jericho, and there the LORD showed him the whole land: . . . . the LORD said to Moses, "This is the land that I promised Abraham, Isaac, and Jacob I would give to their descendants. I have let you see it, but I will not let you go there."

11. Moses died in the land of Moab.

Deuteronomy 34:5-6, 11-12 (page _____ in the Old Testament): So Moses, the LORD's servant, died there in the land of Moab, as the LORD had said he would. The LORD buried him in a valley in Moab, opposite the town of Bethpeor, but to this day no one knows the exact place of his burial....No other prophet has ever done miracles and wonders like those that the LORD sent Moses to perform against the king of Egypt, his officials, and the entire country. No other prophet has been able to do the great and terrifying things that Moses did in the sight of all Israel.

12. Jesus is the perfect sacrifice, ONCE and for ALL.

Hebrews 9:12 (page _____ in the New Testament): When Christ went through the tent and entered once and for all into the Most Holy Place, He did not take the blood of goats and bulls to offer as a sacrifice; rather, He took His own blood and obtained eternal salvation for us!

Lesson 23

Joshua, the New Leader of the Israelites

God chose Moses to lead His people out of Egypt.

Exodus 3:4-6, 10 (page _____ in the Old Testament). See Lesson 17, #2 and #3.

God had a plan to save the Israelites.

Exodus 12:12-13 (page _____ in the Old Testament). See Lesson 19, #6.

God provided for His people:

i. God led the Israelites with cloud and fire.
   Exodus 13:20-21 (page _____ in the Old Testament): See Lesson 20, #4.

ii. God took the Israelites safely through the Red Sea.
   Exodus 14:21-22 (page _____ in the Old Testament): See Lesson 20, #8.

iii. God gave the Israelites water and food.
   Exodus 15:22-27; Exodus 16:1-36 (page _____ in the Old Testament): See Lesson 20, #10.

God spoke laws (commandments) for the Israelites.

Exodus 20:1-17 (page _____ in the Old Testament): See Lesson 21, #8.

Moses disobeyed God.

Numbers 20:7-12 (page _____ in the Old Testament): See Lesson 22, #8.

1. **God chose Joshua to succeed Moses.**

   Joshua 1:1-2 (page _____ in the Old Testament): After the death of the LORD's servant Moses, the LORD spoke to Moses' helper, Joshua son of Nun. He said, "My servant Moses is dead. Get ready now, you and all the people of Israel, and cross the Jordan River into the land that I am giving them."

2. **God promised to be with His people.**

   Joshua 1:9 (page _____ in the Old Testament): "Remember that I have commanded you to be determined and confident! Do not be afraid or discouraged, for I, the LORD your God, am with you wherever you go."

3. **The people of Israel crossed the Jordan River.**

   Joshua 3:17 (page _____ in the Old Testament): While the people walked across on dry ground, the priests carrying the LORD's Covenant Box stood on dry ground in the middle of the Jordan until all the people had crossed over.

4. **God kept His promises to His people.**

   Joshua 23:1, 14 (page _____ in the Old Testament): Much later the LORD gave Israel security from their enemies around them. By that time Joshua was very old…."Now my time has come to die. Every one of you knows in his heart and soul that the LORD your God has given you all the good things that He promised. Every promise He made has been kept; not one has failed."

5. **Joshua told the people to choose a god.**

   Joshua 24:14, 15a (page _____ in the Old Testament): "Now then," Joshua continued, "honor the LORD and serve Him sincerely and faithfully. Get rid of the gods which your ancestors used to worship in Mesopotamia and in Egypt, and serve only the LORD. If you are not willing to serve Him, decide today whom you will serve, the gods your ancestors worshiped in Mesopotamia or the gods of the Amorites, in whose land you are now living."

6. **Joshua chose God.**

   Joshua 24:15b (page _____ in the Old Testament): "As for my family and me, we will serve the Lord."

7. **EVERYONE must choose to believe God or not to believe Him.**

   John 3:16-18 (page _____ in the New Testament): For God loved the world so much that He gave His only Son, so that everyone who believes in Him may not die but have eternal life. For God did not send His Son into the world to be its judge, but to be its Savior. Whoever believes in the Son is not judged; but whoever does not believe has already been judged, because he has not believed in God's only Son.

God's Plan of Love

> Write yes or no on the lines:

____ 1. The Lord told Joshua to lead the people of Israel across the Red River.

____ 2. God is always with His people.

____ 3. The people walked across the Jordan River on dry ground.

____ 4. The Lord God gave His people all the good things that He promised.

____ 5. Every promise that God makes to His people, He always keeps.

____ 6. The book of Joshua teaches us that we must honor the Lord and serve Him sincerely and faithfully.

The Egyptians will know that I am the Lord.

Lesson 24

Ruth in God's Plan

1. **Ruth, a woman from Moab, chose the God of the Israelites.**

   Ruth 1:16-17 (page _____ in the Old Testament): But Ruth answered, "Don't ask me to leave you! Let me go with you. Wherever you go, I will go; wherever you live, I will live. Your people will be my people, and your God will be my God. Wherever you die, I will die, and that is where I will be buried. May the LORD's worst punishment come upon me if I let anything but death separate me from you."

2. **Ruth went to the land of the Israelites.**

   Ruth 1:22 (page _____ in the Old Testament): This, then, was how Naomi came back from Moab with Ruth, her Moabite daughter-in-law. When they arrived in Bethlehem, the barley harvest was just beginning.

3. **Ruth worked in the field of Boaz.**

   Ruth 2:3 (page _____ in the Old Testament): So Ruth went out to the fields and walked behind the workers, picking up the heads of grain which they left. It so happened that she was in a field that belonged to Boaz.

God's Plan of Love

4. **Boaz was kind to Ruth.**

   Ruth 2:13 (page _____ in the Old Testament): Ruth answered, "You are very kind to me, sir. You have made me feel better by speaking gently to me, even though I am not the equal of one of your servants."

5. **Boaz married Ruth.**

   Ruth 4:13 (page _____ in the Old Testament): So Boaz took Ruth home as his wife. The LORD blessed her, and she became pregnant and had a son.

6. **God chose Ruth, a woman from Moab, to be an ancestor of Jesus.**

   Matthew 1:1, 6a (page _____ in the New Testament): This is the list of the ancestors of Jesus Christ, a descendant of David, who was a descendant of Abraham. . . . Boaz (his mother was Rahab), Obed (his mother was Ruth). . . .

   God loves ALL people of EVERY nation in the WHOLE WORLD.

   > *John 3:16 (page _____ in the New Testament): For God loved the world so much that He gave His only Son, so that everyone who believes in Him may not die but have eternal life.*

Lesson 25

God Gave Kings to Israel

Ruth and Boaz lived in a time when God ruled Israel through special men called judges.

1. **The people of Israel asked Samuel, who was the judge, for a king.**

   1 Samuel 8:4-5 (page _____ in the Old Testament): Then all the leaders of Israel met together, went to Samuel in Ramah, and said to him, "Look, you are getting old and your sons don't follow your example. So then, appoint a king to rule over us, so that we will have a king, as other countries have."

2. **God chose Saul to be the first king of Israel.**

   1 Samuel 10:23-24 (page _____ in the Old Testament): So they ran and brought Saul out to the people, and they could see that he was a foot taller than anyone else. Samuel said to the people, "Here is the man the LORD has chosen! There is no one else among us like him." All the people shouted, "Long live the king!"

3. **Saul chose his own way. He did not choose God's way.**

   1 Samuel 15:10, 26 (page _____ in the Old Testament): The LORD said to Samuel, "I am sorry that I made Saul king; he has turned away from me and disobeyed my commands." . . . "I will not go back with you," Samuel answered (to Saul). "You rejected the LORD's command, and He has rejected you as king of Israel."

4. **God chose the young man, David, to be the next king of Israel when King Saul died.**

   1 Samuel 16:1, 7b, 12-13 (page _____ in the Old Testament): The LORD said to Samuel, "How long will you go on grieving over Saul? I have rejected him as king of Israel. But now get some olive oil and go to Bethlehem, to a man named Jesse, because I have

God's Plan of Love

chosen one of his sons to be king....Man looks at the outward appearance, but I look at the heart."...So Jesse sent for him (David). He was a handsome, healthy young man, and his eyes sparkled. The LORD said to Samuel, "This is the one—anoint him!" Samuel took the olive oil and anointed David in front of his brothers. Immediately the spirit of the LORD took control of David and was with him from that day on.

5. **David lived with King Saul.**

   1 Samuel 16:21 (page _____ in the Old Testament): David came to Saul and entered his service. Saul liked him very much and chose him as the man to carry his weapons.

6. **The Israelites were at war with their enemies, the Philistines.**

   1 Samuel 17:3 (page _____ in the Old Testament): The Philistines lined up on one hill and the Israelites on another, with a valley between them.

7. **Goliath, a Philistine giant, told the Israelites to choose someone to fight him.**

   1 Samuel 17:8-10 (page _____ in the Old Testament): Goliath stood and shouted at the Israelites, "What are you doing there, lined up for battle? I am a Philistine, you slaves of Saul! Choose one of your men to fight me. If he wins and kills me, we will be your slaves; but if I win and kill him, you will be our slaves. Here and now I challenge the Israelite army. I dare you to pick someone to fight me!"

8. **David said that he would fight Goliath, the Philistine giant.**

   1 Samuel 17:32 (page _____ in the Old Testament): David said to Saul, "Your Majesty, no one should be afraid of this Philistine! I will go and fight him."

9. **David killed Goliath!**

   1 Samuel 17:46a, 47, 50 (page _____ in the Old Testament): "This very day the LORD will put you in my power; I will defeat you.... and everyone here will see that the LORD does not need swords or spears to save His people. He is victorious in battle, and He will put all of you in our power."...And so, without a sword, David defeated and killed Goliath with a sling and a stone!

10. **TODAY God gives us STRENGTH and POWER to do whatever HE asks us to do!**

    Philippians 4:13 (page _____ in the New Testament): I have the strength to face all conditions by the power that Christ gives me.

Part I: God's Plan through the Bible

Lesson 26

David's Sin and God's Forgiveness

1. **David became the king of all Israel.**

   2 Samuel 5:3b, 4-5 (page _____ in the Old Testament): They anointed him (David), and he became king of Israel. David was thirty years old when he became king, and he ruled for forty years. He ruled in Hebron over Judah for seven and a half years, and in Jerusalem over all Israel and Judah for thirty-three years.

2. **God blessed David because he obeyed God.**

   2 Samuel 5:10, 12, 25a (page _____ in the Old Testament): He grew stronger all the time, because the LORD God Almighty was with him….And so David realized that the LORD had established him as king of Israel and was making his kingdom prosperous for the sake of his people….David did what the LORD had commanded.

3. **David loved God, but David sinned.**

   2 Samuel 11:1 (page _____ in the Old Testament): The following spring, at the time of the year when kings usually go to war…David himself stayed in Jerusalem.

   i. David committed adultery with Bathsheba.

   2 Samuel 11:4a (page _____ in the Old Testament): David sent messengers to get her; they brought her to him and he made love to her.

   ii. Bathsheba became pregnant.

   2 Samuel 11:5 (page _____ in the Old Testament): Afterward she discovered that she was pregnant and sent a message to David to tell him.

   iii. David planned the death of Bathsheba's husband, Uriah.

   2 Samuel 11:15, 17b (page _____ in the Old Testament): He wrote: "Put Uriah in the front line, where the fighting is heaviest, then retreat and let him be killed." …Some of David's officers were killed, and so was Uriah.

God's Plan of Love

    iv. David married Bathsheba.

    2 Samuel 11:27 (page _____ in the Old Testament): When the time of mourning was over, David had her brought to the palace; she became his wife and bore him a son. But the LORD was not pleased with what David had done.

4. David repented of his sin.

    i. The Lord sent the prophet Nathan to David.

    2 Samuel 12:1a (page _____ in the Old Testament): The LORD sent the prophet Nathan to David.

    ii. Nathan told David that David had sinned.

    2 Samuel 12:7a (page _____ in the Old Testament): "You are that man," Nathan said to David.

    iii. David confessed his sin.

    2 Samuel 12:13a (page _____ in the Old Testament): "I have sinned against the LORD," David said.

    Psalm 51:1-17 (page _____ in the Old Testament): Be merciful to me, O God, because of Your constant love.

    Because of Your great mercy wipe away my sins!

    Wash away all my evil and make me clean from my sin! I recognize my faults; I am always conscious of my sins.

    I have sinned against You—only against You—and done what You consider evil. So You are right in judging me; You are justified in condemning me.

    I have been evil from the day I was born; from the time I was conceived, I have been sinful. Sincerity and truth are what You require; fill my mind with Your wisdom.

    Remove my sin, and I will be clean; wash me, and I will be whiter than snow.

    Let me hear the sounds of joy and gladness; and though You have crushed and broken me, I will be happy once again. Close Your eyes to my sins and wipe out all my evil.

    Create a pure heart in me, O God, and put a new and loyal spirit in me.

    Do not banish me from Your presence; do not take Your Holy Spirit away from me.

    Give me again the joy that comes from Your salvation, and make me willing to obey You. Then I will teach sinners Your commands, and they will turn back to You.

    Spare my life, O God, and save me, and I will gladly proclaim Your righteousness. Help me to speak, Lord, and I will praise You.

    You do not want sacrifices, or I would offer them; You are not pleased with burnt offerings. My sacrifice is a humble spirit, O God; You will not reject a humble and repentant heart.

iv. God forgave David.

2 Samuel 12:13b (page _____ in the Old Testament): Nathan replied, "The LORD forgives you; you will not die."

5. TODAY we must CONFESS our sins to GOD and REPENT just as David did.

1 John 1:9 (page _____ in the New Testament): But if we confess our sins to God, He will keep His promise and do what is right; He will forgive us our sins and purify us from all our wrongdoing.

Use the letter box below to find these words that were used in the lesson:

love   obey   king   God   sin   David   forgive

Bathsheba   repent   confess

O	Z	N	S	A	W	K	B	Z	A	N	E	O
A	B	W	Y	I	P	I	N	A	I	B	V	A
B	D	E	M	O	N	N	F	H	O	R	L	N
E	E	F	Y	G	G	G	O	B	L	E	U	D
R	D	W	L	A	A	P	R	T	O	P	Z	A
N	L	A	A	F	O	R	G	I	V	E	C	V
A	S	Z	W	B	D	N	I	T	E	N	K	I
C	Q	V	V	V	M	A	V	Z	L	T	Q	D
L	B	A	T	H	S	H	E	B	A	W	Z	S
E	O	D	S	M	U	I	L	O	L	G	H	Y
Z	O	W	T	R	E	B	T	W	S	H	V	N
G	I	L	C	O	N	F	E	S	S	Z	W	D

Lesson 27

Psalms, the Song and Prayer Book of the Bible

The book of Psalms is the song book and prayer book of the Bible. The Psalms were written by different men. David wrote many of the Psalms. There are many kinds of Psalms:

1. **Prayers for forgiveness from God.**

    Psalm 51:1-17 (page _____ in the Old Testament): Be merciful to me, O God, because of Your constant love. Because of Your great mercy wipe away my sins!

    Wash away all my evil and make me clean from my sin!

    I recognize my faults; I am always conscious of my sins.

    I have sinned against You—only against You—and done what You consider evil. So You are right in judging me; You are justified in condemning me.

    I have been evil from the day I was born; from the time I was conceived, I have been sinful. Sincerity and truth are what You require; fill my mind with Your wisdom.

    Remove my sin, and I will be clean; wash me, and I will be whiter than snow.

    Let me hear the sounds of joy and gladness; and though You have crushed me and broken me, I will be happy once again.

    Close Your eyes to my sins and wipe out all my evil.

    Create a pure heart in me, O God, and put a new and loyal spirit in me.

    Do not banish me from Your presence; do not take Your Holy Spirit away from me.

    Give me again the joy that comes from Your salvation, and make me willing to obey You. Then I will teach sinners Your commands, and they will turn back to You.

Spare my life, O God, and save me, and I will gladly proclaim Your righteousness. Help me to speak, Lord, and I will praise You.

You do not want sacrifices, or I would offer them; You are not pleased with burnt offerings. My sacrifice is a humble spirit, O God; You will not reject a humble and repentant heart.

2. **Psalms of trust in God.**

    Psalm 23 (page _____ in the Old Testament):

    The Lord is my Shepherd;

    I have everything I need.

    He lets me rest in fields of green grass and leads me to quiet pools of fresh water. He gives me new strength.

    He guides me in the right paths, as He has promised.

    Even if I go through the deepest darkness, I will not be afraid, LORD, for You are with me. Your shepherd's rod and staff protect me.

    You prepare a banquet for me, where all my enemies can see me; You welcome me as an honored guest and fill my cup to the brim.

    I know that Your goodness and love will be with me all my life; and Your house will be my home as long as I live.

3. **Songs of praise and thanksgiving.**

    Psalm 100 (page _____ in the Old Testament): Sing to the LORD, all the world!

    Worship the LORD with joy; come before Him with happy songs! Acknowledge that the LORD is God.

    He made us, and we belong to Him; we are His people, we are His flock. Enter the Temple gates with thanksgiving; go into its courts with praise. Give thanks to Him and praise Him.

    The LORD is good, His love is eternal and His faithfulness lasts forever.

Lesson 28

God Fulfilled His Promises

1. **All of the Bible tells one story. It is the story of God's love for ALL PEOPLE through His Son, Jesus.**

2. **God carried out His plan of love through:**
    i. Adam and Eve—the first family.
    ii. Abraham—the patriarch.
    iii. Moses—the deliverer, law-giver, and judge.
    iv. Ruth—a woman from Moab.
    v. David—a king.

3. **In the Old TESTAMENT God used prophets to tell His promises for His Son, Jesus, to be born. The NEW TESTAMENT tells how God's promises were fulfilled:**

Old Testament Promises	New Testament Fulfillment
Isaiah 11:10 (page _____ in the Old Testament): The prophet Isaiah said: A day is coming when the new king from the royal line of David will be a Symbol to the nations. They will gather in His royal city and give Him honor.	*John 3:16 (page _____ in the New Testament): For God loved the world so much that He gave His only Son, so that everyone who believes in Him may not die but have eternal life.*

Isaiah 7:14 (page _____ in the Old Testament): The prophet Isaiah said: "Well then, the LORD Himself will give a sign: a woman who is pregnant will have a Son and will name Him Immanuel."	*Matthew 1:20-23 (page _____ in the New Testament): While he was thinking about this, an angel of the LORD appeared to him in a dream and said, "Joseph, descendant of David, do not be afraid to take Mary to be your wife. For it is by the Holy Spirit that she has conceived. She will have a Son, and you will name Him Jesus—because He will save His people from their sins." Now all this happened in order to make come true what the LORD had said through the prophet, "A virgin will become pregnant and have a Son, and He will be called Immanuel," (which means, "God is with us").*
Micah 5:2 (page _____ in the Old Testament): The prophet Micah said: "The LORD says, 'Bethlehem Ephrathah, you are one of the smallest towns in Judah, but out of you I will bring a Ruler for Israel, whose family line goes back to ancient times.'"	*Matthew 2:5-6 (page _____ in the New Testament): "In the town of Bethlehem in Judea," they answered. "For this is what the prophet wrote: 'Bethlehem in the land of Judah, you are by no means the least of the leading cities of Judah; for from you will come a Leader Who will guide my people Israel.'"*
Isaiah 9:6-7 (page _____ in the Old Testament): The prophet Isaiah said: "A Child is born to us! A Son is given to us! And He will be our Ruler. He will be called, 'Wonderful Counselor,' 'Mighty God,' 'Eternal Father,' 'Prince of Peace.' His royal power will continue to grow; His kingdom will always be at peace. He will rule as King David's successor, basing His power on right and justice, from now until the end of time. The LORD Almighty is determined to do all this."	*Luke 1:32-33 (page _____ in the New Testament): "He will be great and will be called the Son of the Most High God. The LORD God will make Him a king, as His ancestor David was, and He will be the King of the descendants of Jacob forever; His kingdom will never end!"*
Isaiah 61:1-3 (page _____ in the Old Testament): The prophet Isaiah said: "The Sovereign LORD has filled me with His spirit. He has chosen me and sent me to	*Luke 4:16-21 (page _____ in the New Testament): Then Jesus went to Nazareth, where He had been brought up, and on the Sabbath He went as usual to the synagogue.*

God's Plan of Love

bring good news to the poor; to heal the broken-hearted, to announce release to captives and freedom to those in prison. He has sent me to proclaim that the time has come when the LORD will save His people and defeat their enemies. He has sent me to comfort all who mourn, to give to those who mourn in Zion joy and gladness instead of grief. They will be like trees that the LORD Himself has planted. They will all do what is right, and God will be praised for what he has done."	*He stood up to read the Scriptures and was handed the book of the prophet Isaiah. He unrolled the scroll and found the place where it is written, "The Spirit of the LORD is upon me, because He has chosen me to bring good news to the poor. He has sent me to proclaim liberty to the captives and recovery of sight to the blind, to set free the oppressed and announce that the time has come when the LORD will save His people." Jesus rolled up the scroll, gave it back to the attendant, and sat down. All the people in the synagogue had their eyes fixed on Him, as he said to them, "This passage of Scripture has come true today, as you heard it being read."*

God made promises before His Son, Jesus, was born. ALL of God's promises were fulfilled in the life of Jesus. Jesus helped people when He was on the earth. Jesus helps people today.

> *Romans 10:10-13 (page _____ in the New Testament): For it is by our faith that we are put right with God; it is by our confession that we are saved. The Scripture says, "Whoever believes in Him will not be disappointed." This includes everyone, because there is no difference between Jews and Gentiles; God is the same LORD of all and richly blesses all who call to Him. As the Scripture says, "Everyone who calls out to the LORD for help will be saved."*

Part I: God's Plan through the Bible

Lesson 29

God Fulfilled His Promises (Continued)

The Old Testament gave God's promises that His Son, Jesus, would be born, that He would die, and that He would live again!

The New Testament tells how God's promises about Jesus were fulfilled!

Old Testament Promises	New Testament Fulfillment
Isaiah 53:4a (page _____ in the Old Testament): The prophet Isaiah said: "But He endured the suffering that should have been ours, the pain that we should have borne."	*1 Peter 2:22-23 (page _____ in the New Testament): He committed no sin, and no one ever heard a lie come from His lips. When He was insulted, He did not answer back with an insult; when He suffered, He did not threaten, but placed His hope in God, the righteous Judge.*
Isaiah 53:7-8 (page _____ in the Old Testament): The prophet Isaiah said: "He was treated harshly, but endured it humbly; He never said a word. Like a Lamb about to be slaughtered, like a sheep about to be sheared, He never said a word. He was arrested and sentenced and led off to die, and no one cared about His fate. He was put to death for the sins of our people."	*1 Peter 2:24-25 (page _____ in the New Testament): Christ Himself carried our sins in His body to the cross, so that we might die to sin and live for righteousness. It is by His wounds that you have been healed. You were like sheep that had lost their way, but now you have been brought back to follow the Shepherd and Keeper of your souls.*
Isaiah 53:9-12 (page _____ in the Old Testament): The prophet Isaiah said: "He was placed in a grave with evil men, He was buried with the rich, even though He had never committed a crime or ever told	*Matthew 27:57-60 (page _____ in the New Testament): When it was evening, a rich man from Arimathea arrived; his name was Joseph, and he also was a disciple of Jesus. He went into the presence of Pilate*

87

God's Plan of Love

a lie." The LORD says, "It was my will that He should suffer; His death was a sacrifice to bring forgiveness. And so He will see His descendants; He will live a long life, and through Him My purpose will succeed. After a life of suffering, He will again have joy; He will know that He did not suffer in vain. My devoted Servant, with Whom I am pleased, will bear the punishment of many and for His sake I will forgive them. And so I will give Him a place of honor, a place among great and powerful men. He willingly gave His life and shared the fate of evil men. He took the place of many sinners and prayed that they might be forgiven."	and asked for the body of Jesus. Pilate gave orders for the body to be given to Joseph. So Joseph took it, wrapped it in a new linen sheet, and placed it in his own tomb, which he had just recently dug out of solid rock. Then he rolled a large stone across the entrance to the tomb and went away.
Psalm 16:9-10 (page _____ in the Old Testament): King David, the prophet, said: "And so I am thankful and glad, and I feel completely secure, because You protect me from the power of death. I have served You faithfully, and You will not abandon Me to the world of the dead."	*Acts 2:30-32 (page _____ in the New Testament):* "He was a prophet, and he knew what God had promised him: God had made a vow that He would make one of David's descendants a king, just as David was. David saw what God was going to do in the future, and so he spoke about the resurrection of the Messiah when he said, 'He was not abandoned in the world of the dead; His body did not rot in the grave.' God has raised this very Jesus from death, and we are all witnesses to this fact."
Psalm 47:5 (page _____ in the Old Testament): The Psalmist said: "God goes up to His throne. There are shouts of joy and the blast of trumpets, as the LORD goes up."	*Mark 16:19-20 (page _____ in the New Testament):* After the Lord Jesus had talked with them, He was taken up to heaven and sat at the right side of God. The disciples went and preached everywhere, and the Lord worked with them and proved that their preaching was true by the miracles that were performed.

God's purpose for sending His Son, Jesus, is told in Isaiah 53:6 (page _____ in the Old Testament):

All of us were like sheep that were lost, each of us going his own way. But the LORD made the punishment fall on Him, the punishment all of us deserved.

Jesus was born to fulfill God's plan to forgive sins and to save sinners.

Luke 19: 10 (page _____ in the New Testament): The Son of Man came to seek and to save the lost.

Lesson 30

God Continues His Plan in the New Testament

The New Testament can be divided into four parts:

Gospels, history, letters, and prophecy.

The Gospels tell the life of Jesus.

The history book tells the history of the church.

The letters tell how to live the Christian life.

The book of prophecy tells of events that will happen.

All of the Old Testament tells about the coming of Jesus. All of the New Testament tells about the life of Jesus on earth and what happened after He returned to the Father.

Jesus Christ is the center of the Bible.
Jesus of Nazareth, the promised Messiah!
The Son of God!
The Saviour!
Our Redeemer and our Lord!
The Bible tells that He HAS come! He IS here!
"There is the Lamb of God, Who takes away the sin of the world!"

John 1:29 (page _____ in the New Testament)

God had a plan to show His love to ALL people of the world!

John 3:16 (page _____ in the New Testament): For God loved the world so much that He gave His only Son, so that everyone who believes in Him may not die but have eternal life.

Lesson 31

Mary Chose God's Plan

God had a plan to show His love for ALL people of the world. He promised to send His Son, Jesus. God fulfilled His promise.

Galatians 4:4-5 (page _____ in the New Testament): But when the right time finally came, God sent His own Son. He came as the Son of a human mother and lived under the Jewish law, to redeem those who were under the law, so that we might become God's sons.

1. **The angel spoke to Mary. He told Mary that she would be the mother of Jesus.**

    Luke 1:30-31 (page _____ in the New Testament): The angel said to her, "Don't be afraid, Mary; God has been gracious to you. You will become pregnant and give birth to a Son and you will name Him Jesus."

2. **Mary did not understand the angel's message.**

    Luke 1:34 (page _____ in the New Testament): Mary said to the angel, "I am a virgin. How, then, can this be?"

3. **The angel explained God's plan to Mary.**

    Luke 1:35, 37 (page _____ in the New Testament): The angel answered, "The Holy Spirit will come on you, and God's power will rest upon you. For this reason the Holy Child will be called the Son of God. . . . For there is nothing that God cannot do."

4. **Mary chose to obey God's plan for her life.**

    Luke 1:38 (page _____ in the New Testament): "I am the Lord's servant," said Mary; "may it happen to me as you have said." And the angel left her.

Part I: God's Plan through the Bible

5. Mary and Joseph were engaged to be married.

Matthew 1:18 (page _____ in the New Testament): This was how the birth of Jesus Christ took place. His mother Mary was engaged to Joseph, but before they were married, she found out that she was going to have a baby by the Holy Spirit.

6. The angel spoke to Joseph. He told Joseph that Mary would be the mother of Jesus.

Matthew 1:20-21 (page _____ in the New Testament): While he was thinking about this, an angel of the Lord appeared to him in a dream and said, "Joseph, descendant of David, do not be afraid to take Mary to be your wife. For it is by the Holy Spirit that she has conceived. She will have a Son, and you will name Him Jesus—because He will save His people from their sins."

7. Joseph chose God's plan for his life.

Matthew 1:24 (page _____ in the New Testament): So when Joseph woke up, he married Mary, as the angel of the Lord had told him to.

8. God fulfilled His Old Testament promises.

Matthew 1:22-23 (page _____ in the New Testament): Now all this happened in order to make come true what the Lord had said through the prophet, "A virgin will become pregnant and have a Son, and He will be called Immanuel" (which means, "God with us").

Isaiah 7:14 (page _____ in the Old Testament): Well then, the Lord Himself will give you a sign: a young woman who is pregnant will have a Son and will name Him "Immanuel."

God ALWAYS keeps His promises.

Romans 4:20-21 (page _____ in the New Testament): His faith did not leave him (Abraham), and he did not doubt God's promise; his faith filled him with power, and he gave praise to God. He was absolutely sure that God would be able to do what He had promised.

When we choose to obey God, we become a part of His plan.

Ephesians 1:13-14 (page _____ in the New Testament): And you also became God's people when you heard the true message, the Good News that brought you salvation. You believed in Christ, and God put His stamp of ownership on you by giving you the Holy Spirit He had promised. The Spirit is the guarantee that we shall receive what God has promised His people, and this assures us that God will give complete freedom to those who are His. Let us praise His glory!

God's Plan of Love

Lesson 32

The Birth of Jesus

> *Galatians 4:4a (page _____ in the New Testament): But when the right time finally came, God sent His own Son.*

1. **The king ordered all people of the world to be counted in their own hometown.**

    Luke 2:1-3 (page _____ in the New Testament): At that time Emperor Augustus ordered a census to be taken throughout the Roman Empire. When this first census took place, Quirinius was the governor of Syria. Everyone, then, went to register himself, each to his own hometown.

2. **Mary and Joseph went from Nazareth to Bethlehem.**

    Luke 2:4-5 (page _____ in the New Testament): Joseph went from the town of Nazareth in Galilee to the town of Bethlehem in Judea, the birthplace of King David. Joseph went there because he was a descendant of David. He went to register with Mary, who was promised in marriage to him.

3. **Jesus was born in Bethlehem.**

    Luke 2:5b-7 (page _____ in the New Testament): She was pregnant, and while they were still in Bethlehem, the time came for her to have her Baby. She gave birth to her first Son, wrapped Him in cloths and laid Him in a manger—there was no room for them to stay in the inn.

4. **The angel told the shepherds that Jesus had been born.**

    Luke 2:8-14 (page _____ in the New Testament): There were some shepherds in that part of the country who were spending the night in the fields, taking care of their flocks. An angel of the Lord appeared to them, and the glory of the Lord shone over them.

They were terribly afraid, but the angel said to them, "Don't be afraid! I am here with good news for you, which will bring great joy to all the people. This very day in David's town your Savior was born—Christ the Lord! And this is what will prove it to you: you will find a baby wrapped in cloths and lying in a manger." Suddenly a great army of heaven's angels appeared with the angel, singing praises to God: "Glory to God in the highest heaven, and peace on earth to those with whom He is pleased!"

5. **The shepherds went to Bethlehem to see Jesus.**

   Luke 2:15-19 (page _____ in the New Testament): When the angels went away from them back into heaven, the shepherds said to one another, "Let's go to Bethlehem and see this thing that has happened, which the Lord has told us." So they hurried off and found Mary and Joseph and saw the Baby lying in the manger. When the shepherds saw Him, they told them what the angel had said about the Child. All who heard it were amazed at what the shepherds said. Mary remembered all these things and thought deeply about them.

6. **The shepherds told other people about Jesus!**

   Luke 2:20 (page _____ in the New Testament): The shepherds went back, singing praises to God for all they had heard and seen; it had been just as the angel had told them.

7. **Wise men from the East visited Jesus.**

   Matthew 2:1-2, 9-11 (page _____ in the New Testament): Jesus was born in the town of Bethlehem in Judea, during the time when Herod was king. Soon afterward, some men who studied the stars came from the East to Jerusalem and asked, "Where is the Baby born to be the King of the Jews? We saw His star when it came up in the East, and we have come to worship Him". . . . And so they left, and on their way they saw the same star they had seen in the East. When they saw it, how happy they were, what joy was theirs! It went ahead of them until it stopped over the place where the Child was. They went into the house, and when they saw the child with His mother Mary, they knelt down and worshiped Him. They brought out their gifts of gold, frankincense, and myrrh, and presented them to Him.

   Philippians 2:6-11 (page _____ in the New Testament): He (Jesus) always had the nature of God, but He did not think that by force He should try to become equal with God. Instead of this, of His own free will, He gave up all He had and took the nature of a servant. He became like man and appeared in human likeness. He was humble and walked the path of obedience all the way to death—His death on the cross. For this reason God raised Him to the highest place above and gave Him the Name that is greater than any other name. And so, in honor of the Name of Jesus all beings in heaven, on earth, and in the world below will fall on their knees, and all will openly proclaim that Jesus Christ is Lord, to the glory of God the Father.

Lesson 33

The Christmas Story

Luke 2:1-20 (page _____ in the New Testament): At that time Emperor Augustus ordered a census to be taken throughout the Roman Empire. When this first census took place, Quirinius was the governor of Syria. Everyone, then, went to register himself, each to his own hometown. Joseph went from the town of Nazareth in Galilee to the town of Bethlehem in Judea, the birthplace of King David. Joseph went there because he was a descendant of David.

He went to register with Mary, who was promised in marriage to him. She was pregnant, and while they were in Bethlehem, the time came for her to have her Baby. She gave birth to her first Son, wrapped Him in cloths and laid Him in a manger—there wasn't room for them to stay in the inn.

There were some shepherds in that part of the country who were spending the night in the fields, taking care of their flocks. An angel of the Lord appeared to them, and the glory of the Lord shone over them. They were terribly afraid, but the angel said to them, "Don't be afraid! I am here with good news for you, which will bring great joy to all the people. This very day in David's town your Savior was born—Christ the Lord! And this is what will prove it to you: you will find a Baby wrapped in cloths and lying in a manger."

Suddenly a great army of heaven's angels appeared with the angel, singing praises to God: "Glory to God in the highest heaven, and peace on earth to those with whom He is pleased!"

When the angels went away from them back into heaven, the shepherds said to one another, "Let's go to Bethlehem and see this thing that has happened, which the Lord has told us."

So they hurried off and found Mary and Joseph and saw the Baby lying in the manger. When the shepherds saw Him, they told them what the angel had said about the Child. All who heard it were amazed at what the shepherds said.

Mary remembered all these things and thought deeply about them.

The shepherds went back, singing praises to God for all they had heard and seen; it had been just as the angel had told them.

Part II:

Jesus: All God and All Man

Lesson 34

Jesus, All God and All Man

Luke 2:40 (page _____ in the New Testament): The Child grew and became strong; He was full of wisdom, and God's blessings were upon Him.

1. **Mary and Joseph took the Baby Jesus to the Temple in Jerusalem.**

   Luke 2:22-23 (page _____ in the New Testament): The time came for Joseph and Mary to perform the ceremony of purification, as the Law of Moses commanded. So they took the Child to Jerusalem to present Him to the Lord, as it is written in the Law of the Lord: "Every first-born male is to be dedicated to the Lord."

2. **Simeon, a man who loved God, lived in Jerusalem.**

   Luke 2:25 (page _____ in the New Testament): At that time there was a man named Simeon living in Jerusalem. He was a good, God-fearing man and was waiting for Israel to be saved.

3. **God had promised Simeon that he would see the Messiah.**

   Luke 2:26 (page _____ in the New Testament): The Holy Spirit was with him and had assured him that he would not die before he had seen the Lord's promised Messiah.

4. **God led Simeon into the Temple.**

   Luke 2:27 (page _____ in the New Testament): Led by the Spirit, Simeon went into the Temple.

5. God fulfilled His promise to Simeon.

Luke 2:28-32 (page _____ in the New Testament): Simeon took the Child in his arms and gave thanks to God "Now, Lord, You have kept Your promise, and You may let Your servant go in peace. With my own eyes I have seen Your Salvation, which You have prepared in the presence of all peoples: A Light to reveal Your will to the Gentiles and bring glory to Your people Israel."

6. Mary and Joseph and Jesus went home to Nazareth.

Luke 2:39-40 (page _____ in the New Testament): When Joseph and Mary had finished doing all that was required by the Law of the Lord, they returned to their hometown of Nazareth in Galilee. The Child grew and became strong; He was full of wisdom, and God's blessings were upon Him.

John 1:14 (page _____ in the New Testament): The Word became a human being and, full of grace and truth, lived among us. We saw His glory, the glory which He received as the Father's only Son.

JESUS WAS ALL GOD AND ALL MAN AT THE VERY SAME TIME!

Lesson 35

The Baptism of Jesus

> *Luke 2:40 (page _____ in the New Testament): The Child grew and became strong; He was full of wisdom, and God's blessings were upon Him.*

1. **Jesus grew physically, mentally, and spiritually.**

    Luke 2:52 (page _____ in the New Testament): Jesus grew both in body and in wisdom, gaining favor with God and men.

2. **Jesus was baptized by John in the Jordan River.**

    Mark 1:9 (page _____ in the New Testament): Not long afterward Jesus came from Nazareth in the province of Galilee, and was baptized by John in the Jordan.

3. **God's Spirit came to Jesus in the form of a dove.**

    Mark 1:10 (page _____ in the New Testament): As soon as Jesus came up out of the water, He saw heaven opening and the Spirit coming down on Him like a dove.

4. **God spoke to Jesus from heaven.**

    Mark 1:11 (page _____ in the New Testament): And a voice came from heaven, "You are My own dear Son. I am pleased with You."

5. **God showed Himself in three ways:**

   In the form of Jesus—God, the Son

   In the form of a dove—God, the Holy Spirit

   In the sound of a voice—God, the Father

   Mark 1:9-11 (page _____ in the New Testament): Not long afterward Jesus came from Nazareth in the province of Galilee, and was baptized by John in the Jordan. As soon as Jesus came up out of the water, He saw heaven opening and the Spirit coming down on Him like a dove. And a voice came from heaven, "You are My own dear Son. I am pleased with You."

   John 10:30 (page _____ in the New Testament): "The Father and I are one."

Lesson 36

The Temptation of Jesus

> *Hebrews 4:15 (page _____ in the New Testament): Our High Priest is not one who cannot feel sympathy for our weaknesses. On the contrary, we have a High Priest who was tempted in every way that we are, but did not sin.*

1. **The Devil/Satan tempted Jesus to use His power for Himself.**

    Matthew 4:1-3 (page _____ in the New Testament): Then the Spirit led Jesus into the desert to be tempted by the Devil. After spending forty days and nights without food, Jesus was hungry. Then the Devil came to Him and said, "If You are God's Son, order these stones to turn into bread."

2. **Jesus chose God's way.**

    Matthew 4:4 (page _____ in the New Testament): But Jesus answered, "The Scripture says, 'Man cannot live on bread alone, but needs every word that God speaks.'"

3. **The Devil/Satan tempted Jesus to use God's power for the wrong reason.**

    Matthew 4:5-6 (page _____ in the New Testament): Then the Devil took Jesus to Jerusalem, the Holy City, set Him on the highest point of the Temple, and said to Him, "If You are God's Son, throw Yourself down, for the Scripture says, 'God will give orders to His angels about You; they will hold You up with their hands, so that not even Your feet will be hurt on the stones.'"

4. **Jesus chose God's way.**

    Matthew 4:7 (page _____ in the New Testament): Jesus answered, "But the Scripture also says, 'Do not put the Lord your God to the test.'"

Part II: Jesus: All God and All Man

5. **The Devil/Satan tempted Jesus to "kneel down and worship me" (Devil).**

   Matthew 4:8-9 (page _____ in the New Testament): Then the Devil took Jesus to a very high mountain and showed Him all the kingdoms of the world in all their greatness. "All this I will give You," the Devil said, "if You kneel down and worship me."

6. **Jesus chose God's way.**

   Matthew 4:10 (page _____ in the New Testament): "Go away, Satan! The Scripture says, 'Worship the Lord your God and serve only Him!'"

7. **Jesus defeated the Devil/Satan with God's Word.**

   Psalm 119:11 (page _____ in the Old Testament): I keep Your law in my heart, so that I will not sin against You.

Jesus was ALL God and ALL man at the VERY SAME TIME!

> *John 14:11 (page _____ in the New Testament):* "BELIEVE ME when I say that I am in the Father and the Father is in Me."

Lesson 37

Why Jesus Came

> *John 10:10b (page _____ in the New Testament):* Jesus said: "I have come in order that you might have life—life in all its fullness."

1. **Jesus went to the synagogue on the Sabbath. He read from the Scriptures written by the prophet Isaiah.**

   Luke 4:16-17 (page _____ in the New Testament): Then Jesus went to Nazareth, where He had been brought up, and on the Sabbath He went as usual to the synagogue. He stood up to read the Scriptures and was handed the book of the prophet Isaiah. He unrolled the scroll and found the place where it is written, . . ."

2. **Jesus used the words of the prophet Isaiah to tell why He came.**

   Luke 4:18-19 (page _____ in the New Testament): "The Spirit of the Lord is upon Me, because He has chosen Me to bring good news to the poor. He has sent Me to proclaim liberty to the captives and recovery of sight to the blind, to set free the oppressed and announce that the time has come when the Lord will save His people."

3. **Jesus said, "This passage of Scripture has come true today, as you heard it being read."**

   Luke 4:20-21 (page _____ in the New Testament): Jesus rolled up the scroll, gave it back to the attendant, and sat down. All the people in the synagogue had their eyes fixed on Him, as He said to them, "This passage of Scripture has come true today, as you heard it being read."

Mission (Luke 4:18-19)	Fulfillment
"The Spirit of the Lord is upon Me."	*Matthew 3:16-17 (page _____ in the New Testament): As soon as Jesus was baptized, He came up out of the water. Then heaven was opened to Him, and He saw the Spirit of God coming down like a dove and lighting on Him. Then a voice said from heaven, "This is My own dear Son, with whom I am pleased."*
"To bring Good News to the poor."	*Matthew 11:28 (page _____ in the New Testament): "Come to Me, all of you who are tired from carrying heavy loads, and I will give you rest."*
"To proclaim liberty to the captives . . . to set free the oppressed."	*Mark 1:23-26 (page _____ in the New Testament): Just then a man with an evil spirit came into the synagogue and screamed, "What do You want with us, Jesus of Nazareth? Are You here to destroy us? I know who You are—You are God's Holy Messenger!" Jesus ordered the spirit, "Be quiet and come out of the man!" The evil spirit shook the man hard, gave a loud scream, and came out of him.*
"Recovery of sight to the blind."	*Matthew 20:30, 34 (page _____ in the New Testament): Two blind men who were sitting by the road heard that Jesus was passing by, so they began to shout, "Son of David! Have mercy on us, Sir!" . . . Jesus had pity on them and touched their eyes; at once they were able to see, and they followed Him.*
To "save His people."	*Mark 10:45 (page _____ in the New Testament): Jesus said: "For even the Son of Man did not come to be served; He came to serve and to give His life to redeem many people."*

> *John 3:16 (page _____ in the New Testament): For God loved the world so much that He gave His only Son, so that everyone who believes in Him may not die but have eternal life.*

God's Plan of Love

Lesson 38

The I AMs of Jesus

John 10:10b (page _____ in the New Testament): Jesus said: "I have come in order that you might have life—life in all its fullness."

1. **Exodus 3:14 (page _____ in the Old Testament): God said, "I am who I am. You must tell them. The One who is called I AM has sent Me to you."**

   Revelation 1:8 (page _____ in the New Testament): "I am the first and the last," says the Lord God Almighty, "who is, who was, and who is to come."

2. **Jesus used word pictures to tell about Himself:**

   i. "I am the bread of life."

      John 6:35 (page _____ in the New Testament): "I am the bread of life," Jesus told them. "He who comes to Me will never be hungry; he who believes in Me will never be thirsty."

   ii. "I am the light of the world."

      John 8:12 (page _____ in the New Testament): Jesus spoke to the Pharisees again. "I am the light of the world," He said. ""Whoever follows Me will have the light of life and will never walk in darkness."

   iii. "I am the gate."

      John 10:9 (page _____ in the New Testament): "I am the gate. Whoever comes in by Me will be saved; he will come in and go out and find pasture."

   iv. "I am the good shepherd."

John 10:11 (page _____ in the New Testament): "I am the good shepherd, who is willing to die for the sheep."

  v. "I am the vine."

John 15:5 (page _____ in the New Testament): "I am the vine, and you are the branches. Whoever remains in Me, and I in him, will bear much fruit; for you can do nothing without Me."

  vi. "I am the resurrection and the life."

John 11:25-26 (page _____ in the New Testament): Jesus said to her, "I am the resurrection and the life. Whoever believes in Me will live, even though he dies; and whoever lives and believes in Me will never die. Do you believe this?"

John 3:16 (page _____ in the New Testament): For God loved the world so much that He gave His only Son, so that everyone who believes in Him may not die but have eternal life.

Lesson 39

I Am the Way, the Truth, and the Life

> John 10:10b (page _____ in the New Testament): Jesus said: "I have come in order that you might have life—life in all its fullness."

> John 14:1-4 (page _____ in the New Testament): "Do not be worried and upset," Jesus told them. "Believe in God and believe also in Me. There are many rooms in My Father's house, and I am going to prepare a place for you. I would not tell you this if it were not so. And after I go and prepare a place for you, I will come back and take you to Myself, so that you will be where I am. You know the way that leads to the place where I am going."

1. **Thomas questioned Jesus.**

    John 14:5 (page _____ in the New Testament): Thomas asked Jesus: "Lord, we do not know where You are going; so how can we know the way to get there?"

2. **Jesus answered Thomas.**

    John 14:6 (page _____ in the New Testament): Jesus answered Thomas: "I am the way, the truth, and the life; no one goes to the Father except by Me."

3. **Knowing Jesus IS knowing God.**

    John 14:7 (page _____ in the New Testament): "Now that you have known Me," He said to them, "you will know My Father also, and from now on you do know Him and you have seen Him."

4. **Seeing Jesus IS seeing God.**

   John 14:8-9 (page _____ in the New Testament): Philip said to Him, "Lord, show us the Father; that is all we need." Jesus answered, "For a long time I have been with you all; yet you do not know Me, Philip? Whoever has seen Me has seen the Father. Why, then, do you say, 'Show us the Father?'"

5. **Hearing Jesus IS hearing God.**

   John 14:10 (page _____ in the New Testament): "Do you not believe, Philip, that I am in the Father and the Father is in Me? The words that I have spoken to you," Jesus said to His disciples, "do not come from Me. The Father, who remains in Me, does His own work."

> *John 14:6, 11 (page _____ in the New Testament): Jesus said: "I am the way, the truth, and the life. . . . Believe Me when I say that I am in the Father and the Father is in Me. If not, believe because of the things I do."*

Lesson 40

God Is ALL Powerful

> *John 10:10b (page _____ in the New Testament): Jesus said: "I have come in order that you might have life—life in all its fullness."*

1. **Jesus calmed a storm.**

    Mark 4:35-41 (page _____ in the New Testament): On the evening of that same day Jesus said to His disciples, "Let us go across to the other side of the lake." So they left the crowd; the disciples got into the boat in which Jesus was already sitting, and they took Him with them. Other boats were there too. Suddenly a strong wind blew up, and the waves began to spill over into the boat, so that it was about to fill with water. Jesus was in the back of the boat, sleeping with His head on a pillow. The disciples woke Him up and said, "Teacher, don't You care that we are about to die?" Jesus stood up and commanded the wind, "Be quiet!" and He said to the waves, "Be still!" The wind died down, and there was a great calm. Then Jesus said to His disciples, "Why are you frightened? Do you still have no faith?" But they were terribly afraid and began to say to one another, "Who is this man? Even the wind and the waves obey Him!"

2. **Jesus walked on the water.**

    John 6:16-21 (page _____ in the New Testament): When evening came, Jesus' disciples went down to the lake, got into a boat, and went back across the lake toward Capernaum. Night came on, and Jesus still had not come to them. By then a strong wind was blowing and stirring up the water. The disciples had rowed about three or four miles when they saw Jesus walking on the water, coming near the boat, and they were terrified. "Don't be afraid," Jesus told them, "it is I." Then they willingly took Him into the boat, and immediately the boat reached land at the place they were heading for.

3. Jesus changed Zacchaeus' life.

Luke 19:1-9 (page _____ in the New Testament): Jesus went on into Jericho and was passing through. There was a chief tax collector there named Zacchaeus, who was rich. He was trying to see who Jesus was, but he was a little man and could not see Jesus because of the crowd. So he ran ahead of the crowd and climbed a sycamore tree to see Jesus, who was going to pass that way. When Jesus came to that place, He looked up and said to Zacchaeus, "Hurry down, Zacchaeus, because I must stay in your house today." Zacchaeus hurried down and welcomed Him with great joy. All the people who saw it started grumbling, "This man has gone as a guest to the home of a sinner!" Zacchaeus stood up and said to the Lord, "Listen, Sir! I will give half my belongings to the poor, and if I have cheated anyone, I will pay him back four times as much." Jesus said to him, "Salvation has come to this house today, for this man, also, is a descendant of Abraham. The Son of Man came to seek and to save the lost."

> *Colossians 1:15-23a (page _____ in the New Testament): Christ is the visible likeness of the invisible God. He is the first-born Son, superior to all created things. For through Him God created everything in heaven and on earth, . . . God created the whole universe through Him and for Him. . . . At one time you were far away from God and were His enemies because of the evil things you did and thought. But now, by means of the physical death of His Son, God has made you His friends, in order to bring you, holy, pure, and faultless, into His presence. You must, of course, continue faithful on a firm and sure foundation, and must not allow yourselves to be shaken from the hope you gained when you heard the gospel.*

Lesson 41

God Cares

> *John 10:10b (page _____ in the New Testament): Jesus said: "I have come in order that you might have life–life in all its fullness."*

1. **Jesus cared about hungry people.**

    i. Jesus told His disciples to feed the people.

    Luke 9:12-14 (page _____ in the New Testament): When the sun was beginning to set, the twelve disciples came to Him and said, "Send the people away so that they can go to the villages and farms around here and find food and lodging, because this is a lonely place." But Jesus said to them, "You yourselves give them something to eat." They answered, "All we have are five loaves and two fish. Do you want us to go and buy food for this whole crowd?" (There were about five thousand there.) Jesus said to His disciples, "Make the people sit down in groups of about fifty each."

    ii. Jesus blessed the food. The disciples gave the food to the people.

    Luke 9:15-16 (page _____ in the New Testament): After the disciples had done so, Jesus took the five loaves and two fish, looked up to heaven, thanked God for them, broke them, and gave them to the disciples to distribute to the people.

    iii. Jesus provided more food than the people could eat.

    Luke 9:17 (page _____ in the New Testament): They all ate and had enough, and the disciples took up twelve baskets of what was left over.

2. Jesus cared about a paralyzed man.

   i. Some men brought a paralyzed man to Jesus.

   Luke 5:18-19 (page _____ in the New Testament): Some men came carrying a paralyzed man on a bed, and they tried to carry him into the house and put him in front of Jesus. Because of the crowd, however, they could find no way to take him in. So they carried him up on the roof, made an opening in the tiles, and let him down on his bed into the middle of the group in front of Jesus.

   ii. Jesus healed the man.

   Luke 5:20 25 (page _____ in the New Testament): When Jesus saw how much faith they had, He said to the man, "Your sins are forgiven, My friend." The teachers of the Law and the Pharisees began to say to themselves, "Who is this man who speaks such blasphemy! God is the only one who can forgive sins!" Jesus knew their thoughts and said to them, "Why do you think such things? Is it easier to say, 'Your sins are forgiven you,' or to say, 'Get up and walk'? I will prove to you, then, that the Son of Man has authority on earth to forgive sins." So He said to the paralyzed man, "I tell you, get up, pick up your bed, and go home!" At once the man got up in front of them all, took the bed he had been lying on, and went home, praising God.

   iii. The people praised God.

   Luke 5:26 (page _____ in the New Testament): They were all completely amazed! Full of fear, they praised God, saying, "What marvelous things we have seen today!"

3. Jesus cared about many sick people.

Luke 4:40-41 (page _____ in the New Testament): After sunset all who had friends who were sick with various diseases brought them to Jesus; He placed His hands on every one of them and healed them all. Demons also went out from many people, screaming, "You are the Son of God!" Jesus gave the demons an order and would not let them speak, because they knew He was the Messiah.

> *1 Peter 5:7 (page _____ in the New Testament): Leave all your worries with Him, because He cares for you!*

Lesson 42

God Forgives

> *John 10:10b (page _____ in the New Testament): Jesus said: "I have come in order that you might have life–life in all its fullness."*

1. **Jesus went to the home of Simon, a Pharisee, to eat dinner.**

   Luke 7:36 (page _____ in the New Testament): A Pharisee invited Jesus to have dinner with him, and Jesus went to his house and sat down to eat.

2. **A very sinful woman went to Simon's house to see Jesus.**

   Luke 7:37-38 (page _____ in the New Testament): In that town was a woman who lived a sinful life. She heard that Jesus was eating in the Pharisee's house, so she brought an alabaster jar full of perfume and stood behind Jesus, by His feet, crying and wetting His feet with her tears. Then she dried His feet with her hair, kissed them, and poured the perfume on them.

3. **Simon did not understand why Jesus accepted the sinful woman.**

   Luke 7:39 (page _____ in the New Testament): When the Pharisee saw this, he said to himself, "If this man really were a prophet, He would know who this woman is who is touching Him; He would know what kind of sinful life she lives!"

4. **Jesus told Simon a story.**

   Luke 7:40-43 (page _____ in the New Testament): Jesus spoke up and said to him, "Simon, I have something to tell you." "Yes, Teacher," he said, "tell me." "There were two men who owed money to a moneylender," Jesus began. "One owed him five hundred silver coins, and the other owed him fifty. Neither of them could pay him back, so he canceled the debts of both. Which one, then, will love him more?" "I suppose," answered Simon, "that it would be the one who was forgiven more." "You are right," said Jesus.

5. **Jesus told Simon that the sinful woman had shown Him more kindness than Simon had shown Him.**

   Luke 7:44-46 (page _____ in the New Testament): Then He turned to the woman and said to Simon, "Do you see this woman? I came into your home, and you gave Me no water for My feet, but she has washed My feet with her tears and dried them with her hair. You did not welcome Me with a kiss, but she has not stopped kissing My feet since I came. You provided no olive oil for My head, but she has covered My feet with perfume."

6. **The sinful woman came to Jesus because her sins needed to be forgiven.**

   Luke 7:47 (page _____ in the New Testament): "I tell you, then, the great love she has shown proves that her many sins have been forgiven. But whoever has been forgiven little shows only a little love."

7. **Jesus forgave the sinful woman.**

   Luke 7:48 (page _____ in the New Testament): Then Jesus said to the woman, "Your sins are forgiven."

8. **The other people at the dinner table did not understand who Jesus was.**

   Luke 7:49 (page _____ in the New Testament): The others sitting at the table began to say to themselves, "Who is this, who even forgives sins?"

9. **The sinful woman's life was changed because of Jesus.**

   Luke 7:50 (page _____ in the New Testament): But Jesus said to the woman, "Your faith has saved you; go in peace."

Romans 3:23-24 (page _____ in the New Testament): Everyone has sinned and is far away from God's saving presence. But by the free gift of God's grace all are put right with Him through Christ Jesus, who sets them free.

Romans 6:23 (page _____ in the New Testament): For sin pays its wage—death; but God's free gift is eternal life in union with Christ Jesus our Lord.

Lesson 43

God Loves

> *John 10:10b (page _____ in the New Testament): Jesus said: "I have come in order that you might have life–life in all its fullness."*

1. **Jesus loved His friend Lazarus.**

   John 11:5, 14, 17, 33-36, 38-39, 43b, 44 (page _____ in the New Testament): Jesus loved Martha and her sister and Lazarus. . . . Jesus told them (disciples) plainly, "Lazarus is dead. . . . When Jesus arrived, He found that Lazarus had been buried four days before. . . . Jesus saw her (Mary) weeping, and He saw how the people with her were weeping also; His heart was touched, and He was deeply moved. "Where have you buried him?" He asked them. "Come and see, Lord," they answered. Jesus wept. "See how much He loved him!" the people said. . . . Deeply moved once more, Jesus went to the tomb, which was a cave with a stone placed at the entrance. "Take the stone away!" Jesus ordered. . . . He called out in a loud voice, "Lazarus, come out!" He came out, his hands and feet wrapped in grave cloths, and with a cloth around his face. "Untie him," Jesus told them, "and let him go."

"Lazarus, come out!"

Part II: Jesus: All God and All Man

2. **Jesus loved the people of Jerusalem.**

   Matthew 23:37 (page _____ in the New Testament): "Jerusalem, Jerusalem! You kill the prophets and stone the messengers God has sent you! How many times I wanted to put My arms around all your people, just as a hen gathers her chicks under her wings, but you would not let me!"

3. **Jesus loved all the people of the world and gave His life for them.**

   John 3:16 (page _____ in the New Testament): For God loved the world so much that He gave His only Son, so that everyone who believes in Him may not die but have eternal life.

   John 15:12-14 (page _____ in the New Testament): Jesus said: "My commandment is this: Love one another, just as I love you. The greatest love a person can have for his friends is to give his life for them. And you are My friends if you do what I command you."

God's Plan of Love

Lesson 44

God Loves All People

John 10:10b (page _____ in the New Testament): Jesus said: "I have come in order that you might have life–life in all its fullness."

God loves ALL people in ALL of the world.

John 3:16 (page _____ in the New Testament): For God loved the world so much that He gave His only Son, so that everyone who believes in Him may not die but have eternal life.

1. **A teacher of the Law asked Jesus how to have eternal life.**

   Luke 10:25 (page _____ in the New Testament): A teacher of the Law came up and tried to trap Jesus. "Teacher," he asked, "what must I do to receive eternal life?"

2. **Jesus asked the teacher what the Bible said.**

   Luke 10:26 (page _____ in the New Testament): Jesus answered him, "What do the Scriptures say? How do you interpret them?"

3. **The teacher answered Jesus from the Bible:**

   Luke 10:27 (page _____ in the New Testament): "Love the Lord your God with all your heart, strength, and with all your mind; and love your neighbor as you love yourself."

   Deuteronomy 6:5 (page _____ in the Old Testament): "Love the LORD your God with all your heart, with all your soul, and with all your strength."

   Leviticus 19:18b (page _____ in the Old Testament): "Love your neighbor as you love yourself."

4. **The teacher asked Jesus, "Who is my neighbor?"**

   Luke 10:29 (page _____ in the New Testament): But the teacher of the Law wanted to justify himself, so he asked Jesus, "Who is my neighbor?"

5. **Jesus told the teacher a story.**

   Luke 10:30-35 (page _____ in the New Testament): Jesus answered, "There was once a man who was going down from Jerusalem to Jericho when robbers attacked him, stripped him, and beat him up, leaving him half dead. It so happened that a priest was going down that road; but when he saw the man, he walked on by on the other side. In the same way a Levite also came there, went over and looked at the man, and then walked on by on the other side. But a Samaritan who was traveling that way came upon the man, and when he saw him, his heart was filled with pity. He went over to him, poured oil and wine on his wounds and bandaged them; then he put the man on his own animal and took him to an inn, where he took care of him. The next day he took out two silver coins and gave them to the innkeeper, "Take care of him," he told the innkeeper, "and when I come back this way, I will pay you whatever else you spend on him."

6. **Jesus asked the teacher which man acted like a neighbor.**

   Luke 10:36 (page _____ in the New Testament): And Jesus concluded, "In your opinion, which one of these three acted like a neighbor toward the man attacked by the robbers?"

   Luke l0:37a (page _____ in the New Testament): The teacher of the Law answered, "The one who was kind to him."

   Luke 10:37b (page _____ in the New Testament): Jesus replied, "You go, then, and do the same."

God loves ALL people in ALL of the world. God wants US to love ONE ANOTHER!

1 John 4:7-11 (page _____ in the New Testament): Dear friends, let us love one another, because love comes from God. Whoever loves is a child of God and knows God. Whoever does not love does not know God, for God is love. And God showed His love for us by sending His only Son into the world, so that we might have life through Him. This is what love is: it is not that we have loved God, but that He loved us and sent His son to be the means by which our sins are forgiven. Dear friends, if this is how God loved us, then we should love one another.

God loves ALL the people of ALL the world at ALL times; each person must choose to receive God's love or not to receive God's love.

> *Romans 10:12b-13 (page _____ in the New Testament): God is the same Lord of all and richly blesses all who call to Him. As the Scripture says, "Everyone who calls out to the Lord for help will be saved."*

Lesson 45

God Loves Bad People

> *John 10:10b (page _____ in the New Testament):* Jesus said: "I have come in order that you might have life—life in all its fullness."

God loves ALL the people of ALL the world at ALL times. God loves us even before we choose to love Him. Jesus told a story to show how much God loves us.

1. **There was a man who had two sons.**

   Luke 15:11b (page _____ in the New Testament): "There was once a man who had two sons."

2. **The younger son wanted his share of the family property.**

   Luke 15:12 (page _____ in the New Testament): "The younger one said to him, 'Father, give me my share of the property now.' So the man divided his property between his two sons."

3. **The younger son sold his property and left home.**

   Luke 15:13 (page _____ in the New Testament): "After a few days the younger son sold his part of the property and left home with the money. He went to a country far away, where he wasted his money in reckless living."

4. **He spent everything he had.**

   Luke 15:14 (page _____ in the New Testament): "He spent everything he had. Then a severe famine spread over that country, and he was left without a thing."

5. **He got a job feeding the pigs.**

    Luke 15:15-16 (page _____ in the New Testament): "So he went to work for one of the citizens of that country, who sent him out to his farm to take care of the pigs. He wished he could fill himself with the bean pods the pigs ate, but no one gave him anything to eat."

6. **He chose to return to his father.**

    Luke 15:17-20a (page _____ in the New Testament): "At last he came to his senses and said, 'All my father's hired workers have more than they can eat, and here I am about to starve! I will get up and go to my father and say, "Father, I have sinned against God and against you. I am no longer fit to be called your son; treat me as one of your hired workers."' So he got up and started back to his father."

7. **His father welcomed him home.**

    Luke 15:20b (page _____ in the New Testament): "He was still a long way from home when his father saw him; his heart was filled with pity, and he ran, threw his arms around his son, and kissed him."

8. **The son told his father that he was sorry for what he had done.**

    Luke 15:21 (page _____ in the New Testament): "'Father,' the son said, 'I have sinned against God and against you. I am no longer fit to be called your son.'"

9. **The father forgave him.**

    Luke 15:22-24 (page _____ in the New Testament): "But the father called to his servants. 'Hurry!' he said. 'Bring the best robe and put it on him. Put a ring on his finger and shoes on his feet. Then go and get the prize calf and kill it, and let us celebrate with a feast! For this son of mine was dead, but now he is alive; he was lost, but now he has been found.'"

    i. The father showed his love to his son.

    ii. The father accepted his son just as he was.

    iii. The father gave his son special gifts.

    iv. The son received his father's love and his father's gifts.

    v. The father was very happy when his son came home.

Lesson 46

God Loves Good People

John 10:10b (page _____ in the New Testament): Jesus said: "I have come in order that you might have life-life in all its fullness."

God loves ALL the people of ALL the world.

1. **Nicodemus was a good man.**

    John 3:1 (page _____ in the New Testament): There was a Jewish leader named Nicodemus, who belonged to the party of the Pharisees.

    i. He was a leader.

    ii. He was a Pharisee.

2. **Nicodemus went to talk to Jesus.**

    John 3:2 (page _____ in the New Testament): One night he went to Jesus and said to Him, "Rabbi, we know that You are a teacher sent by God. No one could perform the miracles You are doing unless God were with him."

3. **Jesus told Nicodemus that everyone must be born again to be a part of God's plan.**

    John 3:3 (page _____ in the New Testament): Jesus answered, "I am telling you the truth: no one can see the Kingdom of God unless he is born again."

4. Nicodemus did not understand what Jesus told him.

John 3:4 (page _____ in the New Testament): "How can a grown man be born again?" Nicodemus asked. "He certainly cannot enter his mother's womb and be born a second time!"

5. Jesus explained being born again.

John 3:5-8 (page _____ in the New Testament): "I am telling you the truth," replied Jesus, "that no one can enter the Kingdom of God unless he is born of water and the Spirit. A person is born physically of human parents, but he is born spiritually of the Spirit. Do not be surprised because I tell you that you must all be born again. The wind blows wherever it wishes; you hear the sound it makes, but you do not know where it comes from or where it is going. It is like that with everyone who is born of the Spirit."

6. Jesus explained God's plan to love people and for people to love Him.

John 3:14-18 (page _____ in the New Testament): "As Moses lifted up the bronze snake on a pole in the desert, in the same way the Son of Man must be lifted up, so that everyone who believes in Him may have eternal life. For God loved the world so much that He gave His only Son, so that everyone who believes in Him may not die but have eternal life. For God did not send His Son into the world to be its judge, but to be its Savior. Whoever believes in the Son is not judged; but whoever does not believe has already been judged, because he has not believed in God's only Son."

God loves ALL the people of ALL the world. Each person must choose to be a part of God's plan or choose not to be a part of God's plan.

John 3:16 (page _____ in the New Testament): For God loved the world so much that He gave His only Son, so that everyone who believes in Him may not die but have eternal life.

1 John 5:11-12 (page _____ in the New Testament): The testimony is this: God has given us eternal life, and this life has its source in His Son. Whoever has the Son has this life; whoever does not have the Son of God does not have life.

Lesson 47

God Loves Women and Children

John 10:10b (page _____ in the New Testament): Jesus said: "I have come in order that you might have life–life in all its fullness."

1. **God has a plan to love people.**

   > He loves men.
   >
   > He loves women.
   >
   > He loves children.

   Genesis 5:1b-2 (page _____ in the Old Testament): "When God created human beings, He made them like Himself. He created them male and female, blessed them, and named them 'Mankind.'"

2. **God has a special plan for men and women to love each other.**

   Genesis 2:21-24 (page _____ in the Old Testament): Then the LORD God made the man fall into a deep sleep, and while he was sleeping, he took out one of the man's ribs and closed up the flesh. He formed a woman out of the rib and brought her to him. Then the man said, "At last, here is one of my own kind—Bone taken from my bone, and flesh from my flesh. 'Woman' is her name because she was taken out of man." That is why a man leaves his father and mother and is united with his wife, and they become one.

3. **God has a special plan for children.**

   Psalm 127:3 (page _____ in the Old Testament): Children are a gift from the LORD; they are a real blessing.

Ephesians 6:1-4 (page _____ in the New Testament): Children, it is your Christian duty to obey your parents, for this is the right thing to do. "Respect your father and mother" is the first commandment that has a promise added: "so that all may go well with you, and you may live a long time in the land." Parents, do not treat your children in such a way as to make them angry. Instead, raise them with Christian discipline and instruction.

4. **Jesus showed that women are important.**

    Luke 10:38-42 (page _____ in the New Testament): As Jesus and His disciples went on their way, He came to a village where a woman named Martha welcomed Him in her home. She had a sister named Mary, who sat down at the feet of the Lord and listened to His teaching. Martha was upset over all the work she had to do, so she came and said, "Lord, don't you care that my sister has left me to do all the work by myself? Tell her to come and help me!" The Lord answered her, "Martha, Martha! You are worried and troubled over so many things, but just one is needed. Mary has chosen the right thing, and it will not be taken away from her."

    i.   Jesus visited with women.

    ii. Jesus taught women.

    iii. He wanted women to choose to learn from Him.

5. **Jesus showed that children are important. Jesus used a little child to show how to enter God's Kingdom.**

    Matthew 18:2-5 (page _____ in the New Testament): So Jesus called a child, had him stand in front of them, and said, "I assure you that unless you change and become like children, you will never enter the Kingdom of heaven. The greatest in the Kingdom of heaven is the one who humbles himself and becomes like this child. And whoever welcomes in My name one such child as this, welcomes Me."

6. **God has a plan to love people, but people must choose His plan through Jesus Christ.**

    1 Corinthians 1:21-23a (page _____ in the New Testament): For God in His wisdom made it impossible for people to know Him by means of their own wisdom. Instead, by means of the so-called "foolish" message we preach, God decided to save those who believe. Jews want miracles for proof, and Greeks look for wisdom. As for us, we proclaim the crucified Christ.

Part III:

Jesus Teaches Christians How to Live

Lesson 48

Love God

John 10:10b (page _____ in the New Testament): Jesus said: "I have come in order that you might have life—life in all its fullness."

Jesus teaches Christians to love God and to love all people.

Matthew 26:36-40 (page _____ in the New Testament): "Teacher," he asked, "which is the greatest commandment in the Law?" Jesus answered, "Love the Lord your God with all your heart, with all your soul, and with all your mind. This is the greatest and the most important commandment. The second most important commandment is like it: Love your neighbor as you love yourself. The whole Law of Moses and the teachings of the prophets depend on these two commandments."

1. **To love God is to study God's Word/Bible.**

   Luke 24:27 (page _____ in the New Testament): Jesus explained to them what was said about Himself in all the Scriptures, beginning with the books of Moses and the writings of all the prophets.

2. **To love God is to pray.**

   Luke 21:36 (page _____ in the New Testament): "Be on watch and pray always that you will have the strength to go safely through all those things that will happen and to stand before the Son of Man."

3. **To love God is to give.**

   Mark 12:41-44 (page _____ in the New Testament): As Jesus sat near the Temple treasury, He watched the people as they dropped in their money. Many rich men dropped in a lot of money; then a poor widow came along and dropped in two little copper coins, worth about a penny. He called His disciples together and said to them, "I tell you that this poor widow put more in the offering box than all the others. For the others put in what they had to spare of their riches; but she, poor as she is, put in all she had—she gave all she had to live on."

4. **To love God is to worship Him.**

   Matthew 4:10b (page _____ in the New Testament): "The Scripture says, 'Worship the Lord your God and serve only Him.'"

   > *Matthew 5:6 (page _____ in the New Testament): "Happy are those whose greatest desire is to do what God requires; God will satisfy them fully!"*

Part III: Jesus Teaches Christians How to Live

Lesson 49

Love People

John 10:10b (page _____ in the New Testament): Jesus said: "I have come in order that you might have life–life in all its fullness."

Matthew 22:36-40 (page _____ in the New Testament): "Teacher," he asked, "which is the greatest commandment in the Law?" Jesus answered, "Love the Lord your God with all your heart, with all your soul, and with all your mind. This is the greatest and the most important commandment. The second most important commandment is like it: Love your neighbor as you love yourself. The whole Law of Moses and the teachings of the prophets depend on these two commandments."

1. **To love all people is to know that God loves ME!**

    John 3:16 (page _____ in the New Testament): For God loved the world so much that He gave His only Son, so that everyone who believes in Him may not die but have eternal life.

2. **To love people is to help them.**

    Matthew 25:35-36, 40 (page _____ in the New Testament): "I was hungry and you fed Me, thirsty and you gave Me a drink; I was a stranger and you received Me in your homes, naked and you clothed Me; I was sick and you took care of Me, in prison and you visited Me." . . . The King will reply, "I tell you, whenever you did this for one of the least important of these brothers of Mine, you did it for Me!"

3. **To love people is to forgive them.**

   Matthew 5:38-42 (page _____ in the New Testament): "You have heard that it was said, 'An eye for an eye, and a tooth for a tooth.' But now I tell you: do not take revenge on someone who wrongs you. If anyone slaps you on the right cheek, let him slap your left cheek too. And if someone takes you to court to sue you for your shirt, let him have your coat as well. And if one of the occupation troops forces you to carry his pack one mile, carry it two miles. When someone asks you for something, give it to him; when someone wants to borrow something, lend it to him."

4. **To love people is to love your enemies.**

   Matthew 5:43-44 (page _____ in the New Testament): "You have heard that it was said, 'Love your friends, hate your enemies.' But now I tell you: love your enemies and pray for those who persecute you."

   1 John 4:21 (page _____ in the New Testament): The command that Christ has given us is this: whoever loves God must love his brother also.

   > *1 John 3:18 (page _____ in the New Testament):* My children, our love should not be just words and talk; it must be true love, which shows itself in action.

Lesson 50

Tell People

> *John 10:10b (page _____ in the New Testament): Jesus said: "I have come in order that you might have life–life in all its fullness."*

Jesus gave His disciples a special command.

Matthew 28:18-20 (page _____ in the New Testament): Jesus drew near and said to them, "I have been given the authority in heaven and on earth. Go, then, to all peoples everywhere and make them My disciples: baptize them in the name of the Father, the Son, and the Holy Spirit, and teach them to obey everything I have commanded you. And I will be with you always, to the end of the age."

1. **Jesus told His disciples to go everywhere and tell people about Him.**

   Acts 1:8 (page _____ in the New Testament): "But when the Holy Spirit comes upon you, you will be filled with power, and you will be witnesses for Me in Jerusalem, in all of Judea and Samaria, and to the ends of the earth."

   Mark 5:18-20 (page _____ in the New Testament): As Jesus was getting into the boat, the man who had had the demons begged him, "Let me go with you!" But Jesus would not let him. Instead, He told him, "Go back home to your family and tell them how much the Lord has done for you and how kind He has been to you." So the man left and went all through the Ten Towns, telling what Jesus had done for him. And all who heard it were amazed.

God's Plan of Love

2. **Jesus told His disciples to baptize the believers.**

   Acts 2:38 (page _____ in the New Testament): Peter said to them, "Each one of you must turn away from his sins and be baptized in the name of Jesus Christ, so that your sins will be forgiven; and you will receive God's gift, the Holy Spirit."

3. **Jesus told His disciples to teach the believers:**

   i. To be disciples.

   ii. To obey Him.

   John 14:15 (page _____ in the New Testament): "If you love Me, you will obey My commandments."

   > *Matthew 28:20 (page _____ in the New Testament):* "And teach them to obey everything I have commanded you. And I will be with you always, to the end of the age."

Part IV:

Jesus' Death and Resurrection Bring Life in All Its Fullness

Lesson 51

Jesus' Special Supper with His Friends

God showed His love for His friends in a special way. God's friends are those who choose His way, who love Him, and who obey Him. God's friends are called CHRISTIANS.

1. **Jesus was with His friends the night before He died.**

   John 13:1 (page _____ in the New Testament): It was now the day before the Passover Festival. Jesus knew that the hour had come for Him to leave this world and go to the Father. He had always loved those in the world who were His own, and He loved them to the very end.

2. **Jesus and His friends ate the Passover Supper together.**

   John 13:2 (page _____ in the New Testament): Jesus and His disciples were at supper. The Devil had already put into the heart of Judas, the son of Simon Iscariot, the thought of betraying Jesus.

God's Plan of Love

3. **Jesus washed the feet of His friends.**

   John 13:3-5 (page _____ in the New Testament): Jesus knew that the Father had given Him complete power; He knew that He had come from God and was going to God. So He rose from the table, took off His outer garment, and tied a towel around His waist. Then He poured some water into a washbasin and began to wash the disciples' feet and dry them with the towel around His waist.

   i. Jesus showed how He loved His friends.

   ii. Jesus showed how He wants His friends to love one another.

   Philippians 2:6-8 (page _____ in the New Testament): He always had the nature of God, but He did not think that by force He should try to become equal with God. Instead of this, of His own free will He gave up all He had, and took the nature of a servant. He became like man and appeared in human likeness. He was humble and walked the path of obedience all the way to death—His death on the cross.

4. **Jesus gave new meaning to the Passover Supper. Jesus gave a new way to observe the Passover Supper. Christians call this observance the LORD'S SUPPER.**

   i. The bread that Jesus broke and gave His friends was a picture of His death.

   Matthew 26:26 (page _____ in the New Testament): While they were eating, Jesus took a piece of bread, gave a prayer of thanks, broke it, and gave it to His disciples. "Take and eat it," He said, "this is My body."

   ii. The wine in the cup that Jesus gave His friends was a picture of His blood that He shed on the cross.

   Matthew 26:27-28 (page _____ in the New Testament): Then He took a cup, gave thanks to God, and gave it to them. "Drink it, all of you," He said; "this is My blood, which seals God's covenant, My blood poured out for many for the forgiveness of sins."

5. **The observance of the LORD'S SUPPER is for Christians today.**

   1 Corinthians 11:23-26 (page _____ in the New Testament): For I received from the Lord the teaching that I passed on to you: that the Lord Jesus, on the night He was betrayed, took a piece of bread, gave thanks to God, broke it, and said, "This is my body, which is for you. Do this in memory of me." In the same way, after the supper He took the cup and said, "This cup is God's new covenant, sealed with my blood. Whenever you drink it, do so in memory of me." This means that every time you eat this bread and drink from this cup you proclaim the Lord's death until He comes.

Part IV: Jesus' Death and Resurrection Bring Life in All Its Fullness

Lesson 52

Jesus in the Garden of Gethsemane

When Jesus and His friends had finished the Lord's Supper, they went to the Mount of Olives.

Matthew 26:30 (page _____ in the New Testament): Then they sang a hymn and went out to the Mount of Olives.

1. **Jesus and His friends went to the Garden of Gethsemane on the Mount of Olives.**

   Luke 22:39 (page _____ in the New Testament): Jesus left the city and went, as He usually did, to the Mount of Olives; and the disciples went with Him.

2. **Jesus went to pray alone.**

   Luke 22:41 (page _____ in the New Testament): Then He went off from them about the distance of a stone's throw and knelt down and prayed.

3. **Jesus prayed that He would not have to die.**

   Luke 22:42a (page _____ in the New Testament): "Father," He said, "if You will, take this cup of suffering away from Me."

God's Plan of Love

4. **Jesus was willing to choose God's way.**

   Luke 22:42b (page _____ in the New Testament): "Not My will, however, but Your will be done."

5. **An angel came to strengthen (help) Jesus when He was crushed with sorrow.**

   Luke 22:43-44 (page _____ in the New Testament): An angel from heaven appeared to Him and strengthened Him. In great anguish He prayed even more fervently; His sweat was like drops of blood falling to the ground.

6. **His friends were tired and went to sleep.**

   Luke 22:45 (page _____ in the New Testament): Rising from His prayer, He went back to the disciples and found them asleep, worn out by their grief.

7. **Jesus was betrayed by His friend Judas.**

   Luke 22:47-48 (page _____ in the New Testament): Jesus was still speaking when a crowd arrived, led by Judas, one of the twelve disciples. He came up to Jesus to kiss Him. But Jesus said, "Judas, is it with a kiss that you betray the Son of Man?"

8. **The friends of Jesus wanted to fight to save His life.**

   Luke 22:49-53 (page _____ in the New Testament): When the disciples who were with Jesus saw what was going to happen, they asked, "Shall we use our swords, Lord?" And one of them struck the High Priest's slave and cut off his right ear. But Jesus said, "Enough of this!" He touched the man's ear and healed him. Then Jesus said to the chief priests and the officers of the Temple guard and the elders who had come there to get Him, "Did you have to come with swords and clubs, as though I were an outlaw? I was with you in the Temple every day, and you did not try to arrest Me. But this is your hour to act, when the power of darkness rules."

Jesus chose God's way. He chose to die on the cross for OUR sins.

> *Philippians 2:8 (page _____ in the New Testament): He was humble and walked the path of obedience all the way to death—His death on the cross.*

> *John 3:16 (page _____ in the New Testament): For God loved the world so much that He gave His only Son, so that everyone who believes in Him may not die but have eternal life!*

Lesson 53

Jesus' Trial

1. **Jesus was arrested by the soldiers and taken to the house of the High Priest.**

    Luke 22:54 (page _____ in the New Testament): They arrested Jesus and took Him away into the house of the High Priest; and Peter followed at a distance.

2. **Peter denied knowing Jesus.**

    Luke 22:55-57 (page _____ in the New Testament): A fire had been lit in the center of the courtyard, and Peter joined those who were sitting around it. When one of the servant women saw him sitting there at the fire, she looked straight at him and said, "This man too was with Jesus!" But Peter denied it, "Woman, I don't even know Him!"

3. **Peter denied knowing Jesus a second time.**

    Luke 22:58 (page _____ in the New Testament): After a little while a man noticed Peter and said, "You are one of them, too!" But Peter answered, "Man, I am not!"

4. **Peter denied knowing Jesus a third time.**

    Luke 22:59-60 (page _____ in the New Testament): And about an hour later another man insisted strongly, "There isn't any doubt that this man was with Jesus, because he also is a Galilean!" But Peter answered, "Man, I don't know what you are talking about!" At once, while he was still speaking, a rooster crowed.

5. **Peter was sorry that he had denied Jesus. He repented.**

    Luke 22:61-62 (page _____ in the New Testament): The Lord turned around and looked straight at Peter, and Peter remembered that the Lord had said to him, "Before the rooster crows tonight, you will say three times that you do not know Me." Peter went out and wept bitterly.

God's Plan of Love

6. **Jesus was mocked and beaten by His guards.**

   Luke 22:63-65 (page _____ in the New Testament): The men who were guarding Jesus made fun of Him and beat Him. They blindfolded Him and asked Him, "Who hit You? Guess!" And they said many other insulting things to Him.

7. **Jesus was questioned by the Jewish religious leaders.**

   i. People told lies about Jesus.

   ii. Jesus did not answer anyone.

   Mark 14:55-61a (page _____ in the New Testament): The Chief Priests and the whole Council tried to find some evidence against Jesus in order to put Him to death, but they could not find any. Many witnesses told lies against Jesus, but their stories did not agree. Then some men stood up and told this lie against Jesus: "We heard Him say, 'I will tear down this Temple which men have made, and after three days I will build one that is not made by men.'" Not even they, however, could make their stories agree. The High Priest stood up in front of them all and questioned Jesus, "Have You no answer to the accusation they bring against You?" But Jesus kept quiet and would not say a word.

8. **The High Priest asked Jesus, "Are You the Messiah?"**

   Mark 14:61b (page _____ in the New Testament): Again the High Priest questioned Him, "Are You the Messiah, the Son of the Blessed God?"

9. **Jesus answered the High Priest, "I AM!"**

   Mark 14:62 (page _____ in the New Testament): "I am," answered Jesus, "and you will all see the Son of Man seated at the right side of the Almighty and coming with the clouds of heaven!"

10. **The religious leaders voted to put Jesus to death.**

    Mark 14:63-64 (page _____ in the New Testament): The High Priest tore His robes and said, "We don't need any more witnesses! You heard His blasphemy. What is your decision?" They all voted against Him: He was guilty and should be put to death.

11. **The religious leaders took Jesus to Pilate, the Roman governor.**

    John 18:28-31 (page _____ in the New Testament): Early in the morning Jesus was taken from Caiaphas' house to the governor's palace. The Jewish authorities did not go inside the palace, for they wanted to keep themselves ritually clean, in order to be able to eat the Passover meal. So Pilate went outside to them and asked, "What do you accuse this man of?" Their answer was, "We would not have brought Him to you if He had not committed a crime." Pilate said to them, "Then you yourselves take Him and try Him according to your own law." They replied, "We are not allowed to put anyone to death."

12. Pilate asked Jesus, "Are You the King of the Jews?"

John 18:33-35 (page _____ in the New Testament): Pilate went back into the palace and called Jesus. "Are You the King of the Jews?" he asked Him. Jesus answered, "Does this question come from you or have others told you about Me?" Pilate answered, "Do You think I am a Jew? It was Your own people and the chief priests who handed You over to me. What have You done?"

13. Jesus told Pilate that His kingdom was not an earthly kingdom.

John 18:36-37 (page _____ in the New Testament): Jesus said, "My kingdom does not belong to this world; if My Kingdom belonged to this world, My followers would fight to keep Me from being handed over to the Jewish authorities. No, My Kingdom does not belong here. So Pilate asked Him, "Are You a king, then?" Jesus answered, "You say that I am a king. I was born and came into the world for one purpose, to speak about the truth. Whoever belongs to the truth listens to Me."

14. Pilate had Jesus whipped to please the Jewish people.

John 19:1-5 (page _____ in the New Testament): Then Pilate took Jesus and had Him whipped. The soldiers made a crown out of thorny branches and put it on His head; then they put a purple robe on Him and came to Him and said, "Long live the King of the Jews!" And they went up and slapped Him. Pilate went back out once more and said to the crowd, "Look, I will bring Him out here to let you see that I cannot find any reason to condemn Him." So Jesus came out, wearing the crown of thorns and the purple robe. Pilate said to them, "Look! Here is the Man!"

15. The people wanted Jesus to be killed.

John 19:6-7 (page _____ in the New Testament): When the chief priests and the Temple guards saw Him, they shouted, "Crucify Him! Crucify Him!" Pilate said to them, "You take Him, then, and crucify Him. I find no reason to condemn Him." The crowd answered back, "We have a law that says He ought to die, because He claimed to be the Son of God."

God's Plan of Love

16. Pilate said that he had the power to kill Jesus or to set Him free.

John 19:8-10 (page _____ in the New Testament): When Pilate heard this, he was even more afraid. He went back into the palace and asked Jesus, "Where do You come from?" But Jesus did not answer. Pilate said to Him, "You will not speak to me? Remember, I have the authority to set you free and also to have You crucified."

17. Jesus answered Pilate's question.

John 19:11a (page _____ in the New Testament): Jesus answered, "You have authority over Me only because it was given to you by God."

18. Pilate wanted to set Jesus free.

John 19:12-14 (page _____ in the New Testament): When Pilate heard this, he tried to find a way to set Jesus free. But the crowd shouted back, "If you set Him free, that means that you are not the Emperor's friend! Anyone who claims to be a king is a rebel against the Emperor!" When Pilate heard these words, he took Jesus outside and sat down on the judge's seat in the place called "The Stone Pavement." (In Hebrew the name is "Gabbatha.") It was then almost noon of the day before the Passover. Pilate said to the people, "Here is your king!"

19. The people shouted back to Pilate, "Kill Him!"

John 19:15 (page _____ in the New Testament): They shouted back, "Kill Him! Kill Him! Crucify Him!" Pilate asked them, "Do you want me to crucify your king?" The chief priests answered, "The only king we have is the Emperor!"

20. Pilate handed Jesus over to the crowd.

John 19:16 (page _____ in the New Testament): Then Pilate handed Jesus over to them to be crucified. So they took charge of Jesus.

Part IV: Jesus' Death and Resurrection Bring Life in All Its Fullness

Lesson 54

Jesus' Death on the Cross

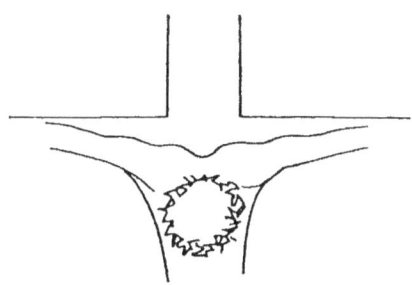

John 3:16 (page _____ in the New Testament): For God loved the world so much that He gave His only Son, so that everyone who believes in Him may not die but have eternal life.

1. **Jesus carried His own cross to a place called Golgotha where the soldiers crucified Him.**

   John 19:17-18 (page _____ in the New Testament): He went out, carrying His cross, and came to "The Place of the Skull," as it is called. (In Hebrew it is called "Golgotha.") There they crucified Him, and they also crucified two other men, one on each side, with Jesus between them.

2. **Pilate placed a sign on the cross of Jesus.**

   John 19:19-22 (page _____ in the New Testament): Pilate wrote a notice and had it put on the cross. "Jesus of Nazareth, the King of the Jews," is what he wrote. Many people read it, because the place where Jesus was crucified was not far from the city. The notice was written in Hebrew, Latin, and Greek. The chief priests said to Pilate, "Do

143

God's Plan of Love

not write 'The King of the Jews', but rather, 'This Man said, I am the King of the Jews.'" Pilate answered, *"What I have written stays written."*

3. **The soldiers gambled for His robe.**

    John 19:23-24 (page _____ in the New Testament): After the soldiers had crucified Jesus, they took His clothes and divided them into four parts, one part for each soldier. They also took the robe, which was made of one piece of woven cloth without any seams in it. The soldiers said to one another, "Let's not tear it; let's throw dice to see who will get it." This happened in order to make the Scripture come true: "They divided My clothes among themselves and gambled for My robe." And this is what the soldiers did.

4. **Jesus made seven statements while He was on the cross.**

    i. Jesus prayed for the people who killed Him.

    Luke 23:34 (page _____ in the New Testament): Jesus said, "Forgive them, Father! They don't know what they are doing."

    ii. Jesus told John to care for His mother.

    John 19:25-27 (page _____ in the New Testament): Standing close to Jesus' cross were his mother, His mother's sister, Mary the wife of Clopas, and Mary Magdalene. Jesus saw His mother and the disciple He loved standing there; so He said to His mother, "He is your son." Then He said to the disciple, "She is your mother." From that time the disciple took her to live in His home.

    iii. Jesus forgave the robber who repented.

    Luke 23:39-43 (page _____ in the New Testament): One of the criminals hanging there hurled insults at Him: "Aren't You the Messiah? Save Yourself and us!" The other one, however, rebuked him, saying, "Don't you fear God? You received the same sentence He did. Ours, however, is only right, because we are getting what we deserve for what we did; but He has done no wrong." And he said to Jesus, "Remember me, Jesus, when You come as King!" Jesus said to him, "I promise you that today you will be in Paradise with Me."

    iv. Jesus was forsaken by God.

    Mark 15:33-34 (page _____ in the New Testament): At noon the whole country was covered with darkness, which lasted for three hours. At three o'clock Jesus cried out with a loud shout, "ELOI, ELOI, LEMA SABACHTHANI?"—which means, "My God, My God, why did You abandon Me?"

    v. Jesus was thirsty.

    John 19:28-29 (page _____ in the New Testament): Jesus knew that by now everything had been completed; and in order to make the Scripture come true, He

Part IV: Jesus' Death and Resurrection Bring Life in All Its Fullness

said, "I am thirsty." A bowl was there, full of cheap wine; so a sponge was soaked in the wine, put on a stalk of hyssop, and lifted up to His lips.

vi. Jesus knew that His earthly ministry was finished.

John 19:30 (page _____ in the New Testament): Jesus drank the wine and said, "It is finished!" Then He bowed His head and gave up His spirit.

vii. Jesus gave His life.

Luke 23:46 (page _____ in the New Testament): Jesus cried out in a loud voice, "Father! In Your Hands I place My spirit!" He said this and died.

5. When Jesus died many wonderful and strange things happened.

Matthew 27:45, 51-53 (page _____ in the New Testament): At noon the whole country was covered with darkness, which lasted for three hours. Then the curtain hanging in the Temple was torn in two from top to bottom. The earth shook, the rocks split apart, the graves broke open, and many of God's people who had died were raised to life. They left the graves, and after Jesus rose from death, they went into the Holy City, where many people saw them.

6. Some of the soldiers who crucified Jesus believed in Him.

Matthew 27:54 (page _____ in the New Testament): When the army officer and the soldiers with him who were watching Jesus saw the earthquake and everything else that happened, they were terrified and said, "He really was the Son of God!"

7. Jesus was buried.

i. Joseph of Arimathea asked Pilate for the body of Jesus.

Matthew 27:57-58 (page _____ in the New Testament): When it was evening, a rich man from Arimathea arrived; his name was Joseph, and he also was a disciple of Jesus. He went into the presence of Pilate and asked for the body of Jesus. Pilate gave orders for the body to be given to Joseph.

ii. Joseph and Nicodemus buried Jesus.

John 19:39-42 (page _____ in the New Testament): Nicodemus, who at first had gone to see Jesus at night, went with Joseph, taking with him about one hundred pounds of spices, a mixture of myrrh and aloes. The two men took Jesus' body and wrapped it in linen cloths with the spices according to the Jewish custom of preparing a body for burial. There was a garden in the place where Jesus had been put to death, and in it there was a new tomb where no one had ever been buried. Since it was the day before the Sabbath and because the tomb was close by, they placed Jesus' body there.

God's Plan of Love

iii. Mary Magdalene and the other Mary were watching.

Mark 15:47 (page _____ in the New Testament): Mary Magdalene and Mary the mother of Jesus were watching and saw where the body of Jesus was placed.

iv. The Pharisees asked Pilate to seal the tomb.

Matthew 27:62-64 (page _____ in the New Testament): The next day, which was a Sabbath, the chief priests and the Pharisees met with Pilate and said, "Sir, we remember that while that liar was still alive He said, 'I will be raised to life three days later.' Give orders, then, for His tomb to be carefully guarded until the third day, so that His disciples will not be able to go and steal the body, and then tell the people that He was raised from death. This last lie would be even worse than the first one."

v. Pilate ordered a seal and a guard for the tomb.

Matthew 27:65-66 (page _____ in the New Testament): "Take a guard," Pilate told them; go and make the tomb as secure as you can." So they left and made the tomb secure by putting a seal on the stone and leaving the guard on watch.

Romans 5:8 (page _____ in the New Testament): But God has shown us how much He loves us—it was while we were still sinners that Christ died for us!

Lesson 55

The Lord Is Risen

> *The LORD is risen!*
>
> *The LORD is risen indeed!!*
>
> *HE is NOT here!!*
>
> *The LORD is risen from the dead!*
>
> *Hallelujah!! Hallelujah!!*

1. **Early Sunday morning, two women went to the tomb of Jesus. They were special friends of Jesus.**

    Matthew 28:1 (page _____ in the New Testament): After the Sabbath, as Sunday morning was dawning, Mary Magdalene and the other Mary went to look at the tomb.

2. **An angel of the Lord came from heaven and rolled the stone away from the tomb.**

    Matthew 28:2-3 (page _____ in the New Testament): Suddenly there was a violent earthquake; an angel of the Lord came down from heaven, rolled the stone away, and sat on it. His appearance was like lightning, and his clothes were white as snow.

3. **The Roman guards were very frightened.**

    Matthew 28:4 (page _____ in the New Testament): The guards were so afraid that they trembled and became like dead men.

4. **The angel said to the women:**

    i. You must not be afraid.

    ii. Jesus is NOT here—HE IS RISEN!

    iii. Go tell His disciples that HE IS RISEN FROM THE DEAD!

    Matthew 28:5-7 (page _____ in the New Testament): The angel spoke to the women. "You must not be afraid," he said. "I know you are looking for Jesus, who was crucified. He is not here; He has been raised, just as He said. Come here and see the place where He was lying. Go quickly now, and tell His disciples, 'He has been raised from death, and now He is going to Galilee ahead of you; there you will see Him!' Remember what I have told you."

5. **The women were very excited! They ran to tell the disciples.**

    Matthew 28:8 (page _____ in the New Testament): So they left the tomb in a hurry, afraid and yet filled with joy, and ran to tell His disciples.

    Matthew 28:9-10 (page _____ in the New Testament): Jesus met the women and said: "Peace be with you." They came up to Him, took hold of His feet, and worshiped Him. "Do not be afraid," Jesus said to them. "Go and tell My brothers to go to Galilee, and there they will see Me."

    > *John 14:27 (page _____ in the New Testament): "Peace is what I leave with you; it is My own peace that I give you. I do not give it as the world does. Do not be worried and upset; do not be afraid."*

Lesson 56

Jesus' Last Days on Earth

Many people saw Jesus after His resurrection.

Jesus gave His friends important instructions.

Jesus went back to heaven.

1. **Thomas saw Jesus. He believed that Jesus was the Risen Lord.**

    i. Thomas had not seen Jesus since His resurrection.

    John 20:24-25 (page _____ in the New Testament): One of the twelve disciples, Thomas (called the Twin), was not with them when Jesus came. So the other disciples told him, "We have seen the Lord!" Thomas said to them, "Unless I see the scars of the nails in His hands and put my finger on those scars and my hand in His side, I will not believe."

    ii. Thomas was with the other disciples when Jesus came and stood among them.

    John 20:26-27 (page _____ in the New Testament): A week later the disciples were together again indoors, and Thomas was with them. The doors were locked, but Jesus came and stood among them and said, "Peace be with you." Then He said to Thomas, "Put your finger here, and look at My hands; then reach out your hand and put it in My side. Stop your doubting, and believe!"

    John 20:28 (page _____ in the New Testament): Thomas said to Jesus: "My Lord and my God!"

    John 20:29 (page _____ in the New Testament): Jesus said to Thomas: "Do you believe because you see Me? How happy are those who believe without seeing Me."

2. **Jesus cooked breakfast for seven of His disciples.**

   John 21:9-13 (page _____ in the New Testament): When they stepped ashore, they saw a charcoal fire there with fish on it and some bread. Then Jesus said to them, "Bring some of the fish you have just caught." Simon Peter went aboard and dragged the net ashore full of big fish, a hundred and fifty-three in all; even though there were so many, still the net did not tear. Jesus said to them, "Come and eat." None of the disciples dared ask Him, "Who are You?" because they knew it was the Lord. So Jesus went over, took the bread, and gave it to them; He did the same with the fish.

3. **Jesus and Peter had a special talk.**

   John 21:15-17 (page _____ in the New Testament): After they had eaten, Jesus said to Simon Peter, "Simon, son of John, do you love Me more than these others do?"

   "Yes, Lord," he answered, "You know that I love You."

   Jesus said to him, "Take care of My lambs."

   A second time Jesus said to him, "Simon son of John, do you love Me?" "Yes, Lord," he answered, "You know that I love You."

   Jesus said to him, "Take care of my sheep."

   A third time Jesus said, "Simon son of John, do you love Me?"

   Peter became sad because Jesus asked him the third time, "Do you love Me?" and so he said to Him, "Lord, You know everything; You know that I love you!"

   Jesus said to him, "Take care of My sheep."

   Peter had denied Jesus three times.

   Jesus asked Peter three times, "Do you love Me?" Peter answered Jesus three times, "Yes, Lord!"

   Jesus wanted Peter to know that he was forgiven.

4. **All the promises about Jesus came true in His life, in His death, and in His resurrection.**

   Luke 24:44-46 (page _____ in the New Testament): Then He said to them, "These are the very things I told you about while I was still with you: everything written about me in the Law of Moses, the writings of the prophets, and the Psalms had to come true." Then He opened their minds to understand the Scriptures, and said to them, "This is what is written: the Messiah must suffer and must rise from death three days later."

Part IV: Jesus' Death and Resurrection Bring Life in All Its Fullness

5. Jesus gave His disciples a special command.

Luke 24:47-49 (page _____ in the New Testament): "In His [Jesus'] name the message about repentance and the forgiveness of sins must be preached to all nations, beginning in Jerusalem. You are witnesses of these things. And I Myself will send upon you what My Father has promised. But you must wait in the city until the power from above comes down upon you."

Matthew 28:18-20 (page _____ in the New Testament): Jesus drew near and said to them, "I have been given all authority in heaven and on earth. Go, then, to all peoples everywhere and make them My disciples: baptize them in the name of the Father, the Son, and the Holy Spirit and teach them to obey everything I have commanded you. And I will be with you always, to the end of the age."

Acts 1:8 (page _____ in the New Testament): "But when the Holy Spirit comes upon you, you will be filled with power, and you will be witnesses for Me in Jerusalem, in all of Judea and Samaria, and to the ends of the earth."

6. Jesus went back to heaven.

Luke 24:50-53 (page _____ in the New Testament): Then He led them out of the city as far as Bethany, where He raised His hands and blessed them. As He was blessing them, He departed from them and was taken up into heaven. They worshiped Him and went back into Jerusalem, filled with great joy, and spent all their time in the Temple giving thanks to God.

Lesson 57

The Promise of the Holy Spirit

Jesus gave His disciples a special command.

Luke 24:47-49 (page _____ in the New Testament): "In His [Jesus'] name the message about repentance and the forgiveness of sins must be preached to all nations, beginning in Jerusalem. You are witnesses of these things. And I Myself will send upon you what My Father has promised. But you must wait in the city until the power from above comes down upon you."

1. **Jesus said, "The Father will give you a Helper [the Holy Spirit]."**

   John 14:16 (page _____ in the New Testament): "I will ask the Father, and He will give you another Helper, who will stay with you forever."

2. **The Holy Spirit is the power of God. The Holy Spirit lives within the hearts of people who believe in Jesus and who obey the teachings of Jesus.**

   Acts 1:8 (page _____ in the New Testament): "But when the Holy Spirit comes upon you, you will be filled with power, and you will be witnesses for Me in Jerusalem, in all of Judea and Samaria, and to the ends of the earth."

3. **Jesus said, "The Holy Spirit will teach you everything and make you remember."**

   John 14:26 (page _____ in the New Testament): "The Helper, the Holy Spirit, whom the Father will send in My name, will teach you everything and make you remember all that I have told you."

Part IV: Jesus' Death and Resurrection Bring Life in All Its Fullness

4. **Jesus said, "The Holy Spirit will point out the truth about sin."**

   John 16:8-9 (page _____ in the New Testament): And when He comes, He will prove to the people of the world that they are wrong about sin and about what is right and about God's judgment. They are wrong about sin, because they do not believe in Me.

   i. Sin is choosing my way.

      Isaiah 53:6 (page _____ in the Old Testament): All of us were like sheep that were lost, each of us going his own way. But the LORD made the punishment fall on Him, the punishment all of us deserved.

   ii. Sin brings death.

      Romans 6:23 (page _____ in the New Testament): For sin pays its wage—death.

   iii. Jesus gives life.

      John 3:16 (page _____ in the New Testament): For God loved the world so much that He gave His only Son, so that everyone who believes in Him may not die but have eternal life.

5. **Jesus said, "The Holy Spirit will never leave you."**

   John 14:17 (page _____ in the New Testament): "He is the Spirit, who reveals the truth about God. The world cannot receive Him, because it cannot see Him or know Him. But you know Him, because He remains with you and is in you."

Jesus made promises to His disciples. Those promises are true for Christians today.

> *Ephesians 1:13-14 (page _____ in the New Testament): And you also became God's people when you heard the true message, the Good News that brought you salvation. You believed in Christ, and God put His stamp of ownership on you by giving you the Holy Spirit He had promised. The Spirit is the guarantee that we shall receive what God has promised His people, and this assures us that God will give complete freedom to those who are His. Let us praise His glory!*

Lesson 58

The Coming of the Holy Spirit

Jesus promised that the Father would send the Holy Spirit.

John 14:16-17 (page _____ in the New Testament): "I will ask the Father, and He will give you another Helper, who will stay with you forever. He is the Spirit, who reveals the truth about God. The world cannot receive Him, because it cannot see Him or know Him. But you know Him, because He remains with you and is in you."

1. **Before Jesus was taken up into heaven, He appeared many times to His disciples.**

   Acts 1:3 (page _____ in the New Testament): For forty days after His death He appeared to them many times in ways that proved beyond doubt that He was alive. They saw Him, and he talked with them about the Kingdom of God.

2. **Jesus told His disciples to wait for the gift of the Holy Spirit.**

   Acts 1:4-5 (page _____ in the New Testament): And when they came together, He gave them this order: "Do not leave Jerusalem, but wait for the gift I told you about, the gift My Father promised. John baptized with water, but in a few days you will be baptized with the Holy Spirit."

3. **The believers/disciples were together in one place on the day of Pentecost.**

   Acts 2:1 (page _____ in the New Testament): When the day of Pentecost came, all the believers were gathered together in one place.

4. **The Holy Spirit came in great power to the believers.**

   Acts 2:2-4 (page _____ in the New Testament): Suddenly there was a noise from the sky which sounded like a strong wind blowing, and it filled the whole house where they were sitting. Then they saw what looked like tongues of fire which spread out and touched each person there. They were all filled with the Holy Spirit and began to talk in other languages, as the Spirit enabled them to speak.

5. **The Holy Spirit came to help believers tell about Jesus. (Please read Acts 2:5-13, page _____ in the New Testament).**

    i. People from many countries were in Jerusalem to worship God.

    Acts 2:5 (page _____ in the New Testament): There were Jews living in Jerusalem, religious men who had come from every country in the world.

    ii. Each person heard his own language being spoken.

    Acts 2:11b (page _____ in the New Testament): "All of us hear them speaking in our own languages about the great things that God has done."

    iii. Peter spoke in a loud voice to the crowd.

    Acts 2:14-15, 21-23, 32-33, 39-41 (page _____ in the New Testament): Then Peter stood up with the other eleven apostles and in a loud voice began to speak to the crowd: "Fellow Jews and all of you who live in Jerusalem, listen to me and let me tell you what this means. These people are not drunk, as you suppose; it is only nine o'clock in the morning. . . . 'whoever calls out to the Lord for help will be saved.' Listen to these words, fellow Israelites! Jesus of Nazareth was a man whose divine authority was clearly proven to you by all the miracles and wonders which God performed through Him. You yourselves know this, for it happened here among you. In accordance with His own plan God had already decided that Jesus would be handed over to you; and you killed Him by letting sinful men crucify Him. . . . God has raised this very Jesus from death, and we are all witnesses to this fact. He has been raised to the right side of God, His Father, and has received from Him the Holy Spirit, as He has promised. What you now see and hear is His gift that He has poured out on us. . . . For God's promise was made to you and your children, and to all who are far away—all whom the Lord our God calls to Himself". . . . Peter made his appeal to them and with many other words he urged them, saying, "Save yourselves from the punishment coming on this wicked people!" Many of them believed his message and were baptized, and about three thousand people were added to the group that day.

The Holy Spirit gives power to Christians today so that they can do the special command of Jesus.

> *Acts 1:8 (page _____ in the New Testament): "But when the Holy Spirit comes upon you, you will be filled with power, and you will be witnesses for Me in Jerusalem, in all of Judea and Samaria, and to the ends of the earth."*

Lesson 59

God's Plan to Love People

The Bible tells us that God has a plan to love people and for people to love Him.

John 3:16 (page _____ in the New Testament): For God loved the world so much that He gave His only Son, so that everyone who believes in Him may not die but have eternal life.

1. **God created people to be like Himself.**

    i. God made people so that they could be His friends.

    Genesis 1:26-27 (page _____ in the Old Testament): Then God said, "And now we will make human beings; they will be like us and resemble us. They will have power over the fish, the birds, and all animals, domestic and wild, large and small." So God created human beings, making them to be like Himself. He created them male and female.

    ii. God made people free to choose.

    Genesis 2:15-17 (page _____ in the Old Testament): Then the LORD God placed the man in the Garden of Eden to cultivate it and guard it. He told him, "You may eat the fruit of any tree in the garden, except the tree that gives knowledge of what is good and what is bad. You must not eat the fruit of that tree; if you do, you will die the same day."

2. **People did not choose God's plan.**

    Isaiah 53:6 (page _____ in the Old Testament): "All of us were like sheep that were lost, each of us going his own way. But the LORD made the punishment fall on Him, the punishment all of us deserved."

Part IV: Jesus' Death and Resurrection Bring Life in All Its Fullness

3. **NOT choosing God's plan is SIN.**

   Sin SEPARATES people FROM GOD.

   Separation from God is DEATH!

   Romans 6:23a (page _____ in the New Testament): For sin pays its wage—death.

4. **EVERYONE has sinned. Sin separates us from God.**

   Romans 3:23 (page _____ in the New Testament): Everyone has sinned and is far away from God's saving presence.

5. **NOTHING people can do can bring them back to God.**

   Ephesians 2:8-9 (page _____ in the New Testament): For it is by God's grace that you have been saved through faith. It is not the result of your own efforts, but God's gift, so that no one can boast about it.

   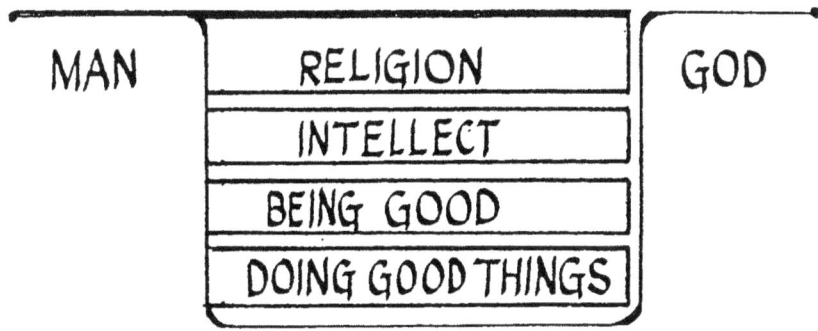

6. **JESUS is the ONLY WAY to bring people back to God.**

   John 14:6 (page _____ in the New Testament): Jesus answered him, "I am the Way, the Truth, and the Life; no one goes to the Father except by Me."

   1 Timothy 2:5-6 (page _____ in the New Testament): For there is one God, and there is One who brings God and mankind together, the man Christ Jesus, who gave Himself to redeem all mankind. That was the proof at the right time that God wants everyone to be saved.

God's Plan of Love

7. **Jesus DIED on the cross.**

   Jesus ROSE from the dead.

   Jesus PAID the PENALTY for the sin OF EVERYONE.

   Romans 5:8-9a (page _____ in the New Testament): But God has shown us how much He loves us—it was while we were still sinners that Christ died for us! By His sacrificial death we are now put right with God.

   1 Peter 2:24 (page _____ in the New Testament): Christ Himself carried our sins in His body to the cross, so that we might die to sin and live for righteousness. It is by His wounds that you have been healed.

   Ephesians 1:6-7 (page _____ in the New Testament): Let us praise God for His glorious grace, for the free gift He gave us in His dear Son! For by the sacrificial death of Christ we are set free, that is, our sins are forgiven. How great is the grace of God!

   > *God made people free to choose.*
   >
   > *Each person must choose God's way—eternal life*
   >
   > *OR choose his own way—eternal death!*

   1 John 5:9-12 (page _____ in the New Testament): We believe man's testimony; but God's testimony is much stronger, and He has given this testimony about His Son. So whoever believes in the Son of God has this testimony in his own heart; but whoever does not believe God, has made a liar of Him, because he has not believed what God has said about His Son. The testimony is this: God has given us eternal life, and this life has its source in His Son. Whoever has the Son has this life; whoever does not have the Son of God does not have life.

Part IV: Jesus' Death and Resurrection Bring Life in All Its Fullness

Lesson 60

God's Plan for People to Love God

God made people free to choose.

Each person must choose God's way—eternal life

OR choose his own way—eternal death!

God loves ALL the people of ALL the world!

Each person must choose to be a part of God's plan

OR choose not to be a part of God's plan!

John 3:16 (page _____ in the New Testament): For God loved the world so much that He gave His only Son, so that everyone who believes in Him may not die but have eternal life.

BELIEVE

Acts 16:30b-31a (page _____ in the New Testament): "Sirs, what must I do to be saved?" They answered, "Believe in the Lord Jesus, and you will be saved."

CONFESS

1 John 1:8-10 (page _____ in the New Testament): If we say that we have no sin, we deceive ourselves, and there is no truth in us. But if we confess our sins to God, He will keep His promise and do what is right: He will forgive us our sins and purify us from all

God's Plan of Love

our wrongdoing. If we say that we have not sinned, we make a liar out of God, and His Word is not in us.

REPENT

Acts 3:19 (page _____ in the New Testament): "Repent, then, and turn to God, so that He will forgive your sins."

ACCEPT BY FAITH

Romans 10:9-13 (page _____ in the New Testament): If you confess that Jesus is Lord and believe that God raised Him from death, you will be saved. For it is by our faith that we are put right with God; it is by our confession that we are saved. The Scripture says, "Whoever believes in Him will not be disappointed." This includes everyone, because there is no difference between Jews and Gentiles; God is the same Lord of all and richly blesses all who call to Him. As the Scripture says, "Everyone who calls out to the Lord for help will be saved."

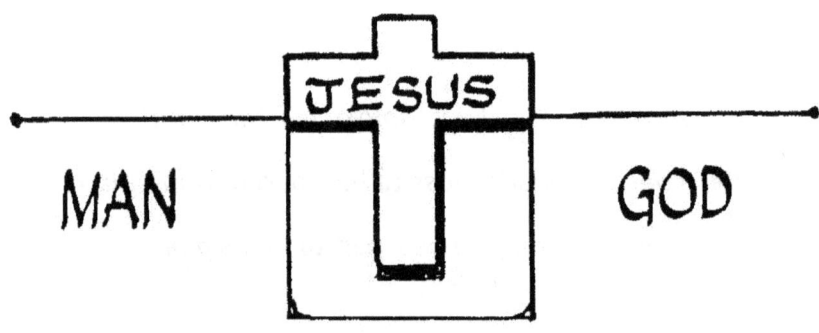

So that we should no longer be slaves of sin.

Lesson 61

God's Plan: Life in All Its Fullness

The International Sunday School Department of First Baptist, Jackson, Mississippi, celebrated its first anniversary with Lesson 61. Each worker told how choosing God's plan had given him/her life in all its fullness.

John 10:10b (page _____ in the New Testament): Jesus said: I have come in order that you might have life—life in all its fullness.

Rene Sugg:

Many years ago I chose God's way. I chose to believe that Jesus is God's Son, that He died for my sin, and that God made Him alive again. This was the first step in my life as a Christian. I was a baby Christian. As a physical baby grows, I have grown spiritually. I have grown by reading the Bible and believing that its commands and promises are for me today. The Bible tells me that Jesus is the answer for every need in my life.

Sometimes I do not feel that God is in my heart, but the Bible tells me that God will never leave me. I trust what the Bible says.

Sometimes I think I cannot do what God wants me to do. But the Bible tells me that I can do all things through God who gives me strength. His strength is mine.

When I do not have wisdom to teach or help people, I remember that the Bible tells me the Holy Spirit is my Teacher and my Helper. He will do God's work through me.

Every day the truth of the Bible means more to me. It tells me that God will give me everything I need because of Jesus Christ.

Frances Smira:

I was reared in a Christian home and attended Sunday School and church with my parents. When I was twelve years old, I accepted Jesus as my Saviour. At that early age, I believed simply that Jesus loved me and that He would make a difference in my life.

Through the years I have had many experiences, some good and some bad, which have shown me again and again that God's love never fails. I realize every day that I do things that do not please Jesus, but He is always willing to forgive me if I just ask.

Even though I have been a Christian many years, I continue to seek God's guidance day by day through praying and studying my Bible.

Bob Smira:

I accepted Jesus as my Saviour when I was twenty-two years old. I was reared in a non-Christian home with a good, loving family. However, I always felt that I needed something more than just daily living. I experienced a great change in my life soon after my marriage to Frances. Frances and her wonderful family had lived with God's love and guidance in a beautiful Christian home for many years. I knew then that I wanted to be a part of God's plan and that I needed to choose God's way.

I did choose God's plan and I was baptized in a small Baptist church in New York City. My life has been blessed with a wonderful wife, a good marriage, two good, beautiful children, six of the best grandchildren anyone could ask for, and also good health.

Life has not always been easy. Ten years ago I was struck down with a severe case of rheumatoid arthritis and thought I would never be able to work or have a normal life because of the pain, anguish, and extreme weakness.

My Jewish doctor, a very knowledgeable, kind, and gentle man, told me that I could choose to stay in bed and turn into a helpless invalid or get up and keep moving, take gold treatments, and recover to a near normal life. I chose the latter. With much help from Frances, my family, and friends, with much pain and great determination, and with a lot of prayers from friends, I was able to continue my work with the Mississippi Air National Guard until retirement.

I thanked God daily for the strength He gave me during those trying times, and I kept in mind that Someone had suffered much, much more than I, as is suggested in John 3:16: God loved the world so much that He gave His only Son, so that everyone who believes in Him may not die but have eternal life.

Last year Frances became ill with the same illness: rheumatoid arthritis. We could hardly believe that the Lord had let this dreadful thing happen to both of us. We had to cope with it and do the best we could. It did make us realize that all the material things, worldly possessions, money, etc., meant nothing to us without our health.

We know that God's great healing power and guidance was ever present. He renewed our strength each day because of the wonderful prayers and help and love of our many friends in this church. The Scripture says, "Believe in the Lord Jesus Christ, and you will be saved—you and your family" (Acts 16:31).

Margaret Price:

I have peace in my heart because I know that Jesus is with me to guide my steps and direct my plans for each day. Jesus helps me to do my best in everything.

Ann Moore:

Jesus Christ makes the difference in my life. My Jesus is love. My Jesus is joy. My Jesus is peace. My Jesus is healing. And my Jesus is strength.

When I talk to Him, He listens. When I read His Word, He teaches me.

Jesus loved me when I could not love myself. He has forgiven me when I could not forgive myself. He is love and His love changes everything.

"The Lord is my Shepherd. I have everything I need" (Psalm 23:1).

Winfred Lott:

Jesus has always been my best friend and my protector. I grew up in the country—on a farm. As a very young boy I learned to work hard. I milked cows very early in the mornings before I went to school. I plowed the fields. I picked cotton. I did not always want to do those chores, but I had to do the work that my father told me to do. As I worked, I learned to pray—to talk to my best friend, Jesus, about everything. He listened as I grumbled about the heat of the sun as I plowed. He listened on those cold winter mornings when I complained about having to get up early to milk cows before going to school. I still had to do my chores, but I felt good because my friend, Jesus, was with me even though I was unhappy and complaining and grumbling.

Jesus was my best friend when I went to Korea as a young soldier during the war. Not only was He my friend, He was my protector. He protected me from the dangers of war. I was wounded, but I survived and returned home to my family. He was my best friend in college. He was my best friend when I was ready to choose a wife and establish a Christian home. Jesus has been my friend in the rearing of our two sons. Jesus is my friend as I travel every week. He protects me from dangers as I travel the highways. He helps me when I have problems in my work. Jesus is my friend and protector. Psalm 91 is the passage from the Bible that I claim for my family and for myself.

Becky Lott:

When I was a little girl I learned to sing a song: "If you want joy, real joy—Let Jesus come into your heart! Your sins He will take away, Your nights He will turn to day, Your life He will make it over anew. If you want joy, real joy—Let Jesus come into your heart!"

I was ten years old when I chose God's way for my life. I asked Jesus to come into my heart. Jesus has given me joy every day. Jesus has given me peace as I have faced life. Joy and peace in times of decision, in times of disappointment, in times of illness, in times of death. Joy and peace in my home, in my work. Jesus said: "Peace is what I leave with you; it is My own peace that I give you. I do not give it as the world does. Do not be worried and upset; do not be afraid" (John 14:27).

Mercedes Cleveland:

As the song says, "Every day with Jesus is sweeter than the day before!" Every day as I read God's Word, He gives me new insight into His teachings. No matter what the day brings, He gives me strength and comfort if I just remember to let HIM have control. Jesus gives my life purpose and direction; He makes my life rich and meaningful. How I praise Him and thank Him for His sacrificial love for all the people in all the world—including me! I pray that I may honor Him daily by sharing that love through service in His name.

Fidelia Campbell:

I was reared in a Christian home. I was thirteen years old when I accepted Jesus Christ as my Saviour. I started reading my Bible, but I did not grow as a Christian should.

Eight years ago some of my dear friends were killed in an automobile accident, and I realized that my life could be taken just that quickly! I realized that I had not been living as a Christian. I asked Jesus to forgive me. He did. Now, I can truly say that Jesus means everything to me. He is my strength, my shield, and my stronghold in times of trouble.

Two of my favorite Scripture verses are, "All things work together for good for those who love the Lord, who are called according to His purpose"

(Romans 8:28), and, "My grace is sufficient for thee, for my strength is made perfect in your weakness. Therefore most gladly I will rather boast in my infirmities that the power of Christ may rest upon me" (2 Corinthians 12:9).

Dr. Joel Alvis:

Each morning when I awake, my assurance (faith) that Jesus Christ is Lord of my life gives me the strength to face or undertake the tasks that are before me that day. Prayer undergirds that strength and gives me the peace and confidence that are necessary each day in my work. My faith makes me a whole or complete person.

Martha Jean Alvis:

For me, Jesus Christ gives both direction and purpose to my life. With Him, I have a way to see the things that happen; I have a way to deal with the circumstances of my life; I have a way to relate to the people I meet; and with Him I know that life has meaning and He has a plan. Jesus Christ is the cement that holds me together, the balm that heals my hurts, the anchor that holds me safe.

Part V:

The People God Chose to Start and Build His Church

Lesson 62

The Beginning of the Church

> *Matthew 16:18b (page _____ in the New Testament): "On this rock foundation I will build My church and not even death will ever be able to overcome it."*

The word church has different meanings:

- a building where believers in Jesus meet to worship
- a local group of believers in Jesus
- all the believers in Jesus.

Jesus started the church.

1. **Jesus asked His disciples a question.**

    Matthew 16:13b (page _____ in the New Testament): Jesus asked His disciples, "Who do people say the Son of Man is?"

2. **The disciples answered that people thought Jesus was one of the prophets.**

    Matthew 16:14 (page _____ in the New Testament): "Some say John the Baptist," they answered. "Others say Elijah, while others say Jeremiah or some other prophet."

    Matthew 16:15b (page _____ in the New Testament): Jesus asked His disciples, "Who do you say I am?"

    Matthew 16:16 (page _____ in the New Testament): Simon Peter answered, "You are the Messiah, the Son of the living God."

God's Plan of Love

3. **Jesus was pleased with Simon Peter's answer.**

   Matthew 16:17 (page _____ in the New Testament): "Good for you, Simon son of John!" answered Jesus. "For this truth did not come to you from any human being, but it was given to you directly by My Father in heaven."

4. **Jesus built the church on people's faith in Him.**

   Matthew 16:18 (page _____ in the New Testament): "And so I tell you, Peter; you are a rock, and on this rock foundation I will build My church and not even death will ever be able to overcome it."

5. **Jesus continues to build the church with believers in Him.**

   Ephesians 2:20-22 (page _____ in the New Testament): You, too, are built upon the foundation laid by the apostles and prophets, the cornerstone being Christ Jesus Himself. He is the One who holds the whole building together and makes it grow into a sacred temple dedicated to the Lord. In union with Him you, too, are being built together with all the others into a place where God lives through His Spirit.

The church continues to grow today with believers in Jesus.

Lesson 63

The Beginning of the Church (Continued)

Acts 2:42 (page   in the New Testament): They [believers in Jesus] spent their time in learning from the apostles, taking part in the fellowship, and sharing in the fellowship meals and the prayers.

1. **Peter preached the story of Jesus on the day of Pentecost.**

    Acts 2:32-33 (page _____ in the New Testament): "God has raised this very Jesus from death, and we are all witnesses to this fact. He has been raised to the right side of God, His Father, and has received from Him the Holy Spirit, as He had promised. What you now see and hear is His gift that He has poured out on us."

2. **Many people believed Peter's message.**

    Acts 2:41 (page _____ in the New Testament): Many of them believed his message and were baptized, and about three thousand people were added to the group that day.

3. **The believers learned together and shared together.**

    Acts 2:42 (page _____ in the New Testament): They spent their time in learning from the apostles, taking part in the fellowship, and sharing in the fellowship meals and the prayers.

    i. They learned about Jesus from the apostles.

    Acts 5:42 (page _____ in the New Testament): And every day in the Temple and in people's homes they continued to teach and preach the Good News about Jesus the Messiah.

    ii. They worshiped God together.

God's Plan of Love

Ephesians 5:19 (page _____ in the New Testament): Speak to one another with the words of psalms, hymns, and sacred songs; sing hymns and psalms to the Lord with praise in your hearts.

iii. They cared for one another.

Acts 2:44-46 (page _____ in the New Testament): All the believers continued together in close fellowship and shared their belongings with one another. They would sell their property and possessions, and distribute the money among all, according to what each one needed. Day after day they met as a group in the Temple, and they had their meals together in their homes, eating with glad and humble hearts.

iv. They prayed together.

Ephesians 6:18 (page _____ in the New Testament): Do all this in prayer, asking for God's help. Pray on every occasion, as the Spirit leads. For this reason keep alert and never give up; pray always for all God's people.

The believers in the church today, should:

i. learn about Jesus,

ii. worship God,

iii. care about one another,

iv. pray together.

Lesson 64

Peter's Call and Answer

Matthew 4:19-20 (page _____ in the New Testament): Jesus said to them, "Come with Me, and I will teach you to catch men." At once they left their nets and went with Him.

1. **Jesus called Peter to follow Him.**

   Matthew 4:18-19 (page _____ in the New Testament): As Jesus walked along the shore of Lake Galilee, He saw two brothers who were fishermen, Simon (called Peter) and his brother Andrew, catching fish in the lake with a net. Jesus said to them, "Come with Me, and I will teach you to catch men."

2. **Peter believed in Jesus and followed him.**

   Matthew 4:20 (page _____ in the New Testament): At once they left their nets and went with Him.

3. **Many people would not follow Jesus because they could not understand His teachings.**

   John 6:66 (page _____ in the New Testament): Because of this, many of Jesus' followers turned back and would not go with Him any more.

   John 6:67 (page _____ in the New Testament): Jesus asked the twelve disciples, "And you—would you also like to leave?"

   John 6:68-69 (page _____ in the New Testament): Simon Peter answered Jesus, "Lord, to whom would we go? You have the words that give eternal life. And now we believe and know that You are the Holy One who has come from God."

Jesus was preparing Peter to help build His church.

> *Matthew 16:18b (page _____ in the New Testament): "And on this rock foundation I will build My church, and not even death will ever be able to overcome it."*

Lesson 65

Peter's Denial and God's Forgiveness

1 Peter 1:3 (page _____ in the New Testament): Let us give thanks to the God and Father of our Lord Jesus Christ! Because of His great mercy He gave us new life by raising Jesus Christ from death. This fills us with a living hope!

1. **Peter sinned. He denied that he knew Jesus.**

    i. Peter followed Jesus to the house of the High Priest.
    Mark 14:66 (page _____ in the New Testament): Peter was still down in the courtyard when one of the High Priest's servant girls came by.

    ii. A servant girl said that Peter was a follower of Jesus.
    Mark 14:67 (page _____ in the New Testament): When she saw Peter warming himself, she looked straight at him and said, "You, too, were with Jesus of Nazareth."

    iii. Peter denied that he knew Jesus.
    Mark 14:68 (page _____ in the New Testament): But he denied it, "I don't know… I don't understand what you are talking about," he answered, and went out into the passageway. Just then a rooster crowed.

    iv. The servant girl repeated that Peter was a follower of Jesus.
    Mark 14:69 (page _____ in the New Testament): The servant girl saw him there and began to repeat to the bystanders, "He is one of them!"

    v. Peter denied that he knew Jesus and the other disciples.
    Mark 14:70a (page _____ in the New Testament): But Peter denied it again.

    vi. The people accused Peter a third time of being a follower of Jesus.
    Mark 14:70b (page _____ in the New Testament): A little while later the bystanders accused Peter again, "You can't deny that you are one of them, because you, too, are from Galilee."

    vii. Peter swore that he did not know Jesus.
    Mark 14:71 (page _____ in the New Testament): Then Peter said, "I swear that I

God's Plan of Love

am telling the truth! May God punish me if I am not! I do not know the Man you are talking about!"

viii. The rooster crowed. Peter remembered what Jesus had said. Peter was very sorry.

Mark 14:72 (page _____ in the New Testament): Just then a rooster crowed a second time, and Peter remembered how Jesus had said to him, "Before the rooster crows two times, you will say three times that you do not know Me." And he broke down and cried.

2. **Jesus forgave Peter.**

   i. Jesus asked Peter, "Do you love Me?"

   John 21:15a (page _____ in the New Testament): After they had eaten, Jesus said to Simon Peter, "Simon son of John, do you love Me more than these others do?"

   ii. Peter answered, "Yes, Lord."

   John 21:15b (page _____ in the New Testament): "Yes, Lord," he answered, "You know that I love You."

   John 21:15c (page _____ in the New Testament): Jesus said to Peter, "Take care of My lambs."

   John 21:16a (page _____ in the New Testament): Jesus asked Peter again, "Simon son of John, do you love Me?"

   iii. Peter answered, "Yes, Lord."

   John 21:16b (page _____ in the New Testament): "Yes, Lord," he answered, "You know that I love You."

   John 21:16c (page _____ in the New Testament): Jesus said to Peter, "Take care of My sheep."

   John 21:17a (page _____ in the New Testament): A third time Jesus said, "Simon son of John, do you love Me?"

   iv. Peter told Jesus again that he loved Him.

   John 21:17b (page _____ in the New Testament): Peter became sad because Jesus asked him the third time, "Do you love Me?" and so he said to Him, "Lord, You know everything; You know that I love You!"

   John 21:17c (page _____ in the New Testament): Jesus said to him, "Take care of My sheep."

Jesus chose Peter to help build His church.

Lesson 66

Peter Began His Assignment to Help Build the Church

Acts 4:20 (page _____ in the New Testament): For we cannot stop speaking of what we ourselves have seen and heard.

> Jesus died on the cross for our sin.
>
> Jesus was buried.
>
> Jesus came back to life.
>
> Jesus gave His disciples His special command.
>
> Jesus ascended to heaven.
>
> The Holy Spirit came to help the believers.

1. **Peter healed a man who could not walk.**

    Acts 3:1-8 (page _____ in the New Testament): One day Peter and John went to the Temple at three o'clock in the afternoon, the hour for prayer. There at the Beautiful Gate, as it was called, was a man who had been lame all his life. Every day he was carried to the gate to beg for money from the people who were going into the Temple. When he saw Peter and John going in, he begged them to give him something. They looked straight at him, and Peter said, "Look at us!" So he looked at them, expecting to get something from them. But Peter said to him, "I have no money at all, but I give you what I have: in the name of Jesus Christ of Nazareth I order you to get up and walk!" Then he took him by his right hand and helped him up. At once the man's feet and ankles became strong; he jumped up, stood on his feet, and started walking around. Then he went into the Temple with them, walking and jumping and praising God.

2. **Peter and John preached about Jesus. Many people believed. The Jewish leaders put Peter and John in jail.**

   Acts 4:1-4 (page _____ in the New Testament): Peter and John were still speaking to the people when some priests, the officer in charge of the Temple guards, and some Sadducees arrived. They were annoyed because the two apostles were teaching the people that Jesus had risen from death, which proved that the dead will rise to life. So they arrested them and put them in jail until the next day, since it was already late. But many who heard the message believed; and the number of men grew to about five thousand.

   Acts 4:7 (page _____ in the New Testament): The Jewish leaders asked Peter and John, "How did you do this? What power do you have or whose name did you use?"

3. **Peter said that he used the power of the name of Jesus to heal the lame man.**

   Acts 4:8-10 (page _____ in the New Testament): Peter, full of the Holy Spirit, answered them, "Leaders of the people and elders: If we are being questioned today about the good deed done to the lame man and how he was healed, then you should all know, and all the people of Israel should know, that this man stands here before you completely well through the power of the name of Jesus Christ of Nazareth—whom you crucified and whom God raised from death."

4. **Peter said that Jesus is the only way to God.**

   Acts 4:12 (page _____ in the New Testament): "Salvation is to be found through Him alone; in all the world there is no one else whom God has given who can save us."

5. **The Jewish leaders told Peter and John NOT to speak in the name of Jesus.**

   Acts 4:18 (page _____ in the New Testament): So they called them back in and told them that under no condition were they to speak or to teach in the name of Jesus.

6. **Peter and John chose to obey God.**

   Acts 4:19-20 (page _____ in the New Testament): But Peter and John answered to them, "You yourselves judge which is right in God's sight—to obey you or to obey God. For we cannot stop speaking of what we ourselves have seen and heard."

7. **Peter and John grew in faith and boldness.**

   Acts 4:31 (page _____ in the New Testament): When they finished praying, the place where they were meeting was shaken. They were all filled with the Holy Spirit and began to proclaim God's message with boldness.

Today believers grow in faith and boldness when they choose to obey God.

Lesson 67

Peter Continued His Assignment to Help Build the Church

Acts 10:34-35 (page _____ in the New Testament): Peter began to speak: "I now realize that it is true that God treats everyone on the same basis. Whoever fears Him and does what is right is acceptable to Him, no matter what race he belongs to."

1. **A Roman soldier named Cornelius was a good man. He and his family worshiped God.**

   Acts 10:1-2 (page _____ in the New Testament): There was a man in Caesarea named Cornelius, who was a captain in the Roman army regiment called "The Italian Regiment." He was a religious man; he and his whole family worshiped God. He also did much to help the Jewish poor people and was constantly praying to God.

2. **Cornelius was told in a vision from God to send for Peter.**

   Acts 10:3-6 (page _____ in the New Testament): It was about three o'clock one afternoon when he had a vision, in which he clearly saw an angel of God come in and say to him, "Cornelius!" He stared at the angel in fear and said, "What is it, sir?" The angel answered, "God is pleased with your prayers and works of charity, and is ready to answer you. And now send some men to Joppa for a certain man whose full name is Simon Peter. He is a guest in the home of a tanner of leather named Simon, who lives by the sea."

3. **Cornelius obeyed God. He sent for Peter.**

   Acts 10:7-8 (page _____ in the New Testament): Then the angel went away, and Cornelius called two of his house servants and a soldier, a religious man who was one of his personal attendants. He told them what had happened and sent them off to Joppa.

God's Plan of Love

4. **Peter also had a vision from God.**

   Acts 10:9-16 (page _____ in the New Testament): The next day, as they were on their way and coming near Joppa, Peter went up on the roof of the house about noon in order to pray. He became hungry and wanted something to eat; while the food was being prepared, he had a vision. He saw heaven opened and something coming down that looked like a large sheet being lowered by its four corners to the earth. In it were all kinds of animals, reptiles, and wild birds. A voice said to him, "Get up, Peter; kill and eat!" But Peter said, "Certainly not, Lord! I have never eaten anything ritually unclean or defiled." The voice spoke to him again, "Do not consider anything unclean that God has declared clean." This happened three times, and then the thing was taken back up into heaven.

5. **Peter did not understand the vision.**

   Acts 10:17-20 (page _____ in the New Testament): While Peter was wondering about the meaning of this vision, the men sent by Cornelius had learned where Simon's house was, and they were now standing in front of the gate. They called out and asked, "Is there a guest here by the name of Simon Peter?" Peter was still trying to understand what the vision meant, when the Spirit said, "Listen! Three men are here looking for you. So get ready and go down, and do not hesitate to go with them, for I have sent them."

6. **Peter obeyed God. He went to see Cornelius.**

   Acts 10:21-23 (page _____ in the New Testament): So Peter went down and said to the men, "I am the man you are looking for. Why have you come?" "Captain Cornelius sent us," they answered. "He is a good man who worships God and is highly respected by all the Jewish people. An angel of God told him to invite you to his house, so that he could hear what you have to say." Peter invited the men in and had them spend the night there. The next day he got ready and went with them; and some of the believers from Joppa went along with him.

The church grows when believers have faith to obey God!

Part V: The People God Chose to Start and Build His Church

Lesson 68

Cornelius Chose to Be a Part of God's Church

Acts 10:34-35 (page _____ in the New Testament): Peter began to speak: "I now realize that it is true that God treats everyone on the same basis. Whoever fears Him and does what is right is acceptable to Him, no matter what race he belongs to."

1. **Peter and some believers went to the house of Captain Cornelius. Cornelius waited with relatives and friends.**

    Acts 10:24 (page _____ in the New Testament): The following day he arrived in Caesarea, where Cornelius was waiting for him, together with relatives and close friends that he had invited.

2. **Cornelius wanted to worship Peter, but Peter would not let him.**

    Acts 10:25-26 (page _____ in the New Testament): As Peter was about to go in, Cornelius met him, fell at his feet, and bowed down before him. But Peter made him rise. "Stand up," he said, "I myself am only a man."

3. **Peter told Cornelius that a Jew is not allowed to visit with Gentiles. Peter asked Cornelius, "Why did you send for me?"**

    Acts 10:27-29 (page _____ in the New Testament): Peter kept on talking to Cornelius as he went into the house, where he found many people gathered. He said to them, "You yourselves know very well that a Jew is not allowed by his religion to visit or associate with Gentiles. But God has shown me that I must not consider any person ritually unclean or defiled. And so when you sent for me, I came without any objection. I ask you, then, why did you send for me?"

4. **Cornelius told Peter about his vision.**

    Acts 10:30-33 (page _____ in the New Testament): Cornelius said, "It was about this time three days ago that I was praying in my house at three o'clock in the afternoon.

181

God's Plan of Love

Suddenly a man dressed in shining clothes stood in front of me and said: 'Cornelius! God has heard your prayer and has taken notice of your works of charity. Send someone to Joppa for a man whose full name is Simon Peter. He is a guest in the home of Simon the tanner of leather, who lives by the sea.' And so I sent for you at once, and you have been good enough to come. Now we are all here in the presence of God, waiting to hear anything that the Lord has instructed you to say."

5. Peter told the people about Jesus.

   i. The Good News of peace through Jesus Christ is for ALL the people of ALL the world.
Acts 10:34-36 (page _____ in the New Testament): Peter began to speak: "I now realize that it is true that God treats everyone on the same basis. Whoever fears Him and does what is right is acceptable to Him, no matter what race he belongs to. You know the message He sent to the people of Israel, proclaiming the Good News of peace through Jesus Christ, who is Lord of all."

   ii. Jesus did many wonderful things in the land of Israel.
Acts 10:37-39a (page _____ in the New Testament): "You know of the great event that took place throughout the land of Israel, beginning in Galilee after John preached his message of baptism. You know about Jesus of Nazareth and how God poured out on Him the Holy Spirit and power. He went everywhere doing good and healing all who were under the power of the Devil, for God was with Him. We are witnesses of everything that He did in the land of Israel and in Jerusalem."

   iii. Jesus died on the cross. God raised Him from the dead.
Acts 10:39b-41 (page _____ in the New Testament): "Then they put Him to death by nailing Him to a cross. But God raised Him from death three days later and caused Him to appear, not to everyone, but only to the witnesses that God had already chosen, that is, to us who ate and drank with Him after He rose from death."

   iv. Jesus told His friends to share the Good News.
Acts 10:42 (page _____ in the New Testament): "And He commanded us to preach the gospel to the people and to testify that He is the one whom God has appointed judge of the living and the dead."

   v. Everyone who believes in Jesus will have his sins forgiven.
Acts 10:43 (page _____ in the New Testament): "All the prophets spoke about Him, saying that everyone who believes in Him will have his sins forgiven through the power of His name."

6. The people who believed Peter's message about Jesus received the Holy Spirit.

Acts 10:44-48 (page _____ in the New Testament): While Peter was still speaking, the Holy Spirit came down on all those who were listening to his message. The Jewish believers who had come from Joppa with Peter were amazed that God had poured out His gift of the Holy Spirit on the Gentiles also. For they heard them speaking in strange tongues and praising God's greatness. Peter spoke up: "These people have received the Holy Spirit, just as we also did. Can anyone, then, stop them from being baptized with water?" So he ordered them to be baptized in the name of Jesus Christ. Then they asked him to stay with them for a few days.

Cornelius was not a Jew.

He was a good man.

He was a religious man.

He did good things.

> *A person CANNOT reach God by*
> *being good*
> *or*
> *being religious*
> *or*
> *doing good things.*

Each person must believe in Jesus.

Each person must believe that:

> *Jesus is God's Son,*
>
> *Jesus died for our sin,*
>
> *God raised Jesus from the dead.*

Each person must confess that he/she:

> *has chosen his own way and not God's way, but now*
> *wants God to forgive his sin and*
> *wants to choose God's way and obey Him.*

God wants ALL the people of ALL the world to be a part of HIS CHURCH.

> *John 3:16 (page _____ in the New Testament): For God loved the world so much that He gave His only Son, so that everyone who believes in Him may not die but have eternal life.*

God's Plan of Love

Lesson 69

Stephen Gave His Life to Help Build the Church

Acts 7:59-60 (page _____ in the New Testament): They kept on stoning Stephen as he called out to the Lord, "Lord Jesus, receive my spirit!" He knelt down and cried out in a loud voice, "Lord! Do not remember this sin against them!" He said this and died.

1. **The people in the church had a quarrel. The quarrel was about money for widows.**

    Acts 6:1 (page _____ in the New Testament): Some time later, as the number of disciples kept growing, there was a quarrel between the Greek-speaking Jews and the native Jews. The Greek-speaking Jews claimed that their widows were being neglected in the daily distribution of funds.

2. **The believers chose seven people to help with the money.**

    Acts 6:2-3 (page _____ in the New Testament): So the twelve apostles called the whole group of believers together and said, "It is not right for us to neglect the preaching of God's Word in order to handle finances. So then, brothers, choose seven men among you who are known to be full of the Holy Spirit and wisdom, and we will put them in charge of this matter."

3. **Stephen was one of the helpers.**

    i. He was a man full of faith and the Holy Spirit.

    Acts 6:5a (page _____ in the New Testament): The whole group was pleased with the apostles' proposal, so they chose Stephen, a man full of faith and the Holy Spirit.

    ii. He was a man richly blessed by God.

    iii. He was full of power.

    iv. He performed many miracles.

    Acts 6:8 (page _____ in the New Testament): Stephen, a man richly blessed by God and full of power, performed great miracles and wonders among the people.

Part V: The People God Chose to Start and Build His Church

4. **The apostles prayed and preached.**

    Acts 6:4 (page _____ in the New Testament): "We ourselves, then, will give our full time to prayer and the work of preaching."

5. **The church grew.**

    Acts 6:7 (page _____ in the New Testament): And so the Word of God continued to spread. The number of disciples in Jerusalem grew larger and larger, and a great number of priests accepted the faith.

6. **Some of the Jews argued with Stephen.**

    Acts 6:9 (page _____ in the New Testament): But he was opposed by some men who were members of the synagogue of the Freedmen (as it was called), which had Jews from Cyrene and Alexandria. They and other Jews from the provinces of Cilicia and Asia started arguing with Stephen.

7. **The Holy Spirit gave Stephen wisdom.**

    Acts 6:10 (page _____ in the New Testament): But the Spirit gave Stephen such wisdom that when he spoke, they could not refute him.

8. **Some men said bad things about Stephen. The men took Stephen before the Council.**

    Acts 6:11-14 (page _____ in the New Testament): So they bribed some men to say, "We heard him speaking against Moses and against God!" In this way they stirred up the people, the elders, and the teachers of the Law. They seized Stephen and took him before the Council. Then they brought in some men to tell lies about him, "This man," they said, "is always talking against our sacred Temple and the Law of Moses. We heard him say that this Jesus of Nazareth will tear down the Temple and change all the customs which have come down to us from Moses."

9. **Stephen's face was like the face of an angel.**

    Acts 6:15 (page _____ in the New Testament): All those sitting in the Council fixed their eyes on Stephen and saw that his face looked like the face of an angel.

10. **Stephen preached a long sermon about God's plan. God's plan is to love all people and for all people to love Him.**

    Acts 7:1-53 (page _____ in the New Testament): Please read these pages in your Bible.

11. The Council became furious with Stephen.

Acts 7:54 (page _____ in the New Testament): As the members of the Council listened to Stephen, they became furious and ground their teeth at him in anger.

12. Stephen saw God's glory and Jesus.

Acts 7:55-56 (page _____ in the New Testament): But Stephen, full of the Holy Spirit, looked up to heaven and saw God's glory and Jesus standing at the right side of God. "Look!" he said. "I see heaven opened and the Son of Man standing at the right side of God."

13. The Council killed Stephen.

Acts 7:57-59 (page _____ in the New Testament): With a loud cry the Council members covered their ears with their hands. Then they all rushed at him at once, threw him out of the city, and stoned him. The witnesses left their cloaks in the care of a young man named Saul. They kept on stoning Stephen as he called out to the Lord, "Lord Jesus, receive my spirit!"

14. Stephen asked God to forgive the Council members.

Acts 7:60 (page _____ in the New Testament): He knelt down and cried out in a loud voice, "Lord! Do not remember this sin against them:"' He said this and died.

Stephen chose to give his life for God's church.

Today some people choose to give their lives for Jesus and His church.

> *Philippians 1:28-29 (page _____ in the New Testament): Don't be afraid of your enemies; always be courageous, and this will prove to them that they will lose and that you will win, because it is God who gives you the victory. For you have been given the privilege of serving Christ, not only by believing in Him, but also by suffering for Him.*

Part V: The People God Chose to Start and Build His Church

Lesson 70

Philip Helped to Build the Church in Many Places

Acts 8:4 (page _____ in the New Testament): The believers who were scattered went everywhere, preaching the message.

1. **Stephen was killed for preaching about God's plan.**

   Acts 7:59-60 (page _____ in the New Testament): They kept on stoning Stephen as he called out to the Lord, "Lord, Jesus, receive my spirit!" He knelt down and cried out in a loud voice, "Lord! Do not remember this sin against them!" He said this and died.

2. **The believers were persecuted because of Stephen's death. The believers were scattered to many places.**

   Acts 8:1 (page _____ in the New Testament): That very day the church in Jerusalem began to suffer cruel persecution. All the believers, except the apostles, were scattered throughout the provinces of Judea and Samaria.

3. **The believers went to many places preaching about God's plan.**

   Acts 8:4 (page _____ in the New Testament): The believers who were scattered went everywhere, preaching the message.

4. **Philip and Stephen were chosen to be helpers in the church.**

   Acts 6:5a (page _____ in the New Testament): The whole group was pleased with the apostles' proposal, so they chose Stephen, a man full of faith and the Holy Spirit, and Philip.

5. **Philip went to Samaria to preach.**

   Acts 8:5 (page _____ in the New Testament): Philip went to the principal city in Samaria and preached the Messiah to the people there.

6. **God's angel told Philip to go to a certain road.**

   Acts 8:26 (page _____ in the New Testament): An angel of the Lord said to Philip, "Get ready and go south to the road that goes from Jerusalem to Gaza." (This road is not used in modern times.)

7. **Philip obeyed God. An Ethiopian eunuch was on the same road. The Ethiopian official was reading the Bible.**

   Acts 8:27-28 (page _____ in the New Testament): So Philip got ready and went. Now an Ethiopian eunuch, who was an important official in charge of the treasury of the queen of Ethiopia, was on his way home. He had been to Jerusalem to worship God and was going back home in his carriage. As he rode along, he was reading from the book of the prophet Isaiah.

8. **The Holy Spirit told Philip to go to the official's chariot. Philip chose to obey the Holy Spirit. He asked the official, "Do you understand what you are reading?"**

   Acts 8:29-30 (page _____ in the New Testament): The Holy Spirit said to Philip, "Go over to that carriage and stay close to it." Philip ran over and heard him reading from the book of the prophet Isaiah. He asked him, "Do you understand what you are reading?"

9. **The official asked Philip to sit with him and explain what he was reading.**

   Acts 8:31-34 (page _____ in the New Testament): The official replied, "How can I understand unless someone explains it to me?" And he invited Philip to climb up and sit in the carriage with him. The passage of Scripture which he was reading was this:

   "He was like a sheep that is taken to be slaughtered, like a lamb that makes no sound when its wool is cut off. He did not say a word. He was humiliated, and justice was denied Him. No one will be able to tell about His descendants, because His life on earth has come to an end."

   The official asked Philip, "Tell me, of whom is the prophet saying this? Of himself or of someone else?"

10. **Philip told the official the Good News about Jesus.**

    Acts 8:35 (page _____ in the New Testament): Then Philip began to speak; starting from this passage of Scripture, he told him the Good News about Jesus.

11. **The official wanted to be baptized.**

    Acts 8:36-37 (page _____ in the New Testament): As they traveled down the road, they came to a place where there was some water, and the official said, "Here is some water. What is to keep me from being baptized?" Philip said to him, "You may be baptized if you believe with all your heart." "I do," he answered, "I believe that Jesus Christ is the Son of God."

12. Philip baptized the official in the water.

Acts 8:38 (page _____ in the New Testament): The official ordered the carriage to stop, and both Philip and the official went down into the water, and Philip baptized him.

13. The Spirit of the Lord took Philip away.

Acts 8:39 (page _____ in the New Testament): When they came up out of the water, the Spirit of the Lord took Philip away. The official did not see him again, but continued on his way, full of joy.

Acts 8:40 (page _____ in the New Testament): Philip found himself in Azotus; he went on to Caesarea, and on the way he preached the Good News in every town.

God wanted Philip to be a part of His plan.

God told Philip to tell the Good News about Jesus.

Philip obeyed God.

The church grew because Philip obeyed God.

Philip told people about Jesus.

The church grows today when we obey God and tell people the Good News about Jesus.

Lesson 71

Saul: A Very Special Jew

Philippians 3:7 (page _____ in the New Testament): But all those things that I might count as profit I now reckon as loss for Christ's sake.

Acts 22:3-5 (page _____ in the New Testament); Philippians 3:5-6 (page _____ in the New Testament): "I am a Jew, born in Tarsus in Cilicia. . . . I was circumcised when I was a week old. I am an Israelite by birth, of the tribe of Benjamin, a pure-blooded Hebrew. . . . but brought up here in Jerusalem as a student of Gamaliel. I received strict instruction in the Law of our ancestors and was just as dedicated to God as are all of you who are here today. . . . As far as keeping the Jewish Law is concerned, I was a Pharisee. . . . As far as a person can be righteous by obeying the commands of the Law, I was without fault. . . . I persecuted to death the people who followed this Way. I arrested men and women and threw them into prison. The High Priest and the whole Council can prove that I am telling the truth. I received from them letters written to fellow Jews in Damascus, so I went there to arrest these people and bring them back in chains to Jerusalem to be punished."

1. **Saul was born a Roman citizen.**

   Acts 22:27-28 (page _____ in the New Testament): So the commander went to Paul and asked him, "Tell me, are you a Roman citizen?" "Yes," answered Paul. The commander said, "I became one by paying a large amount of money." "But I am one by birth," Paul answered.

2. **Saul was a Jew. He was a member of the tribe of Benjamin.**

3. **Saul was well educated. Saul's teacher was Gamaliel. Gamaliel was one of the greatest teachers in Jewish history.**

4. **Saul was a Pharisee. The Pharisees were the religious leaders of the Jews. The Pharisees had great power over the Jewish people.**

5. **Saul believed that it was right to persecute the believers in the church.**

6. **Saul obeyed all of the Jewish Law. Obeying the Law did not make Saul a happy man.**

   Romans 7:22-24 (page _____ in the New Testament): My inner being delights in the law of God. But I see a different law at work in my body—a law that fights against the law which my mind approves of. It makes me a prisoner to the law of sin which is at work in my body. What an unhappy man I am! Who will rescue me from this body that is taking me to death?

   > *Romans 7:25a (page _____ in the New Testament): THANKS BE TO GOD, WHO DOES THIS THROUGH OUR LORD JESUS CHRIST!*

Part V: The People God Chose to Start and Build His Church

Lesson 72

Saul: A New Person in Christ

> Acts 9:15 (page _____ in the New Testament): The Lord said to him, "Go, because I have chosen him to serve Me, to make My name known to Gentiles and kings and to the people of Israel."

1. **Saul tried to destroy the church.**

   Acts 8:3 (page _____ in the New Testament): But Saul tried to destroy the church; going from house to house, he dragged out the believers, both men and women, and threw them into jail.

2. **Saul started to Damascus to persecute the believers.**

   Acts 9:1-2 (page _____ in the New Testament): In the meantime Saul kept up his violent threats of murder against the followers of the Lord. He went to the High Priest and asked for letters of introduction to the synagogues in Damascus, so that if he should find there any followers of the Way of the Lord, he would be able to arrest them, both men and women, and bring them back to Jerusalem.

3. **Saul met Jesus on the road to Damascus.**

   Acts 9:3-5 (page _____ in the New Testament): As Saul was coming near the city of Damascus, suddenly a light from the sky flashed around him. He fell to the ground and heard a voice saying to him, "Saul, Saul! Why do you persecute Me?" "Who are You, Lord?" he asked.

   "I am Jesus, whom you persecute," the voice said.

"Who are you, Lord?"

192

Part V: The People God Chose to Start and Build His Church

4. Jesus told Saul to go to Damascus.

Acts 9:6 (page _____ in the New Testament): "But get up and go into the city, where you will be told what you must do."

5. Saul chose to obey Jesus.

Acts 9:7-9 (page _____ in the New Testament): The men who were traveling with Saul had stopped, not saying a word; they heard the voice but could not see anyone. Saul got up from the ground and opened his eyes, but could not see a thing. So they took him by the hand and led him into Damascus. For three days he was not able to see, and during that time he did not eat or drink anything.

6. Ananias was a Christian who lived in Damascus. He had a vision from the Lord.

Acts 9:10-12 (page _____ in the New Testament): There was a Christian in Damascus named Ananias. He had a vision in which the Lord said to him, "Ananias!" "Here I am, Lord," he answered. The Lord said to him, "Get ready and go to Straight Street, and at the house of Judas ask for a man from Tarsus named Saul. He is praying, and in a vision he has seen a man named Ananias come in and place his hands on him so that he might see again."

7. Ananias was afraid of Saul.

Acts 9:13-14 (page _____ in the New Testament): Ananias answered, "Lord, many people have told me about this man and about all the terrible things he has done to Your people in Jerusalem. And he has come to Damascus with authority from the chief priests to arrest all who worship You."

8. The Lord spoke to Ananias.

Acts 9:15-16 (page _____ in the New Testament): The Lord told Ananias: "Go, because I have chosen him to serve Me, to make My name known to Gentiles and kings and to the people of Israel. And I Myself will show him all that he must suffer for My sake."

9. Ananias chose to obey the Lord.

Acts 9:17 (page _____ in the New Testament): So Ananias went, entered the house where Saul was, and placed his hands on him. "Brother Saul," he said, "the Lord has sent me—Jesus Himself, who appeared to you on the road as you were coming here. He sent me so that you might see again and be filled with the Holy Spirit."

God's Plan of Love

10. Saul became a new person.

Acts 9:18-20 (page _____ in the New Testament): At once something like fish scales fell from Saul's eyes, and he was able to see again. He stood up and was baptized; and after he had eaten, his strength came back. Saul stayed for a few days with the believers in Damascus. He went straight to the synagogues and began to preach that Jesus was the Son of God.

11. The people were amazed at the change in Saul.

Acts 9:21 (page _____ in the New Testament): All who heard him were amazed and asked, "Isn't he the one who in Jerusalem was killing those who worship that man Jesus? And didn't he come here for the very purpose of arresting those people and taking them back to the chief priests?"

Acts 9:22 (page _____ in the New Testament): But Saul's preaching became even more powerful, and his proofs that Jesus was the Messiah were so convincing that the Jews who lived in Damascus could not answer him.

12. SAUL was important in God's plan.

ANANIAS was important in God's plan.

PEOPLE who obey GOD today are important in God's plan.

Lesson 73

Paul: God's Missionary to the World

> *Acts 26:19 (page _____ in the New Testament):* "And so . . . I did not disobey the vision I had from heaven."

1. **Saul received his message from Jesus.**

   Galatians 1:11-12 (page _____ in the New Testament): Let me tell you, my brothers, that the gospel I preach is not of human origin. I did not receive it from any man, nor did anyone teach it to me. It was Jesus Christ Himself who revealed it to me.

2. **God chose Saul for a special job.**

   Galatians 1:15 (page _____ in the New Testament): But God in His grace chose me even before I was born, and called me to serve Him.

3. **God prepared Saul for his special job.**

   Galatians 1:16-18 (page _____ in the New Testament): And when He decided to reveal His Son to me, so that I might preach the Good News about Him to the Gentiles, I did not go to anyone for advice, nor did I go to Jerusalem to see those who were apostles before me. Instead, I went at once to Arabia, and then I returned to Damascus. It was three years later that I went to Jerusalem to obtain information from Peter, and I stayed with him for two weeks.

God's Plan of Love

4. **Some believers started a church in Antioch.**

    Acts 11:19-21 (page _____ in the New Testament): Some of the Believers who were scattered by the persecution which took place when Stephen was killed went as far as Phoenicia, Cyprus, and Antioch, telling the message to Jews only. But other Believers, men from Cyprus and Cyrene, went to Antioch and proclaimed the message to Gentiles also, telling them the Good News about the Lord Jesus. The Lord's power was with them, and a great number of people believed and turned to the Lord.

5. **The church in Jerusalem sent Barnabas to Antioch.**

    Acts 11:22-24 (page _____ in the New Testament): The news about this reached the church in Jerusalem, so they sent Barnabas to Antioch. When he arrived and saw how God had blessed the people, he was glad and urged them all to be faithful and true to the Lord with all their hearts. Barnabas was a good man, full of the Holy Spirit and faith, and many people were brought to the Lord.

    Acts 11:25 (page _____ in the New Testament): Then Barnabas went to Tarsus to look for Saul.

6. **Barnabas and Saul went to Antioch. They taught the people in the church.**

    Acts 11:26a (page _____ in the New Testament): When he found him, he took him to Antioch, and for a whole year the two met with the people of the church and taught a large group.

    Acts 11:26b (page _____ in the New Testament): It was at Antioch that the Believers were first called Christians.

7. **God chose Barnabas and Saul to be missionaries.**

    Acts 13:1-3 (page _____ in the New Testament): In the church at Antioch there were some prophets and teachers: Barnabas, Simeon (called the Black), Lucius (from Cyrene), Manaen (who had been brought up with Governor Herod), and Saul. While they were serving the Lord and fasting, the Holy Spirit said to them, "Set apart for Me Barnabas and Saul, to do the work to which I have called them." They fasted and prayed, placed their hands on them, and sent them off.

Part V: The People God Chose to Start and Build His Church

8. **Saul's name was changed to Paul.**

   Acts 13:9a (page _____ in the New Testament): Then Saul—also known as Paul—was filled with the Holy Spirit.

9. **Paul chose to obey God. He preached the Good News of Jesus to the world.**

   Acts 26:19-20 (page _____ in the New Testament): "And so . . . I did not disobey the vision I had from heaven. First in Damascus and in Jerusalem and then in the whole country of Israel and among the Gentiles, I preached that they must repent of their sins and turn to God and do the things that would show they had repented."

   Paul and Barnabas preached the Good News of Jesus to the world.

   The same Good News of Jesus is preached around the world today!

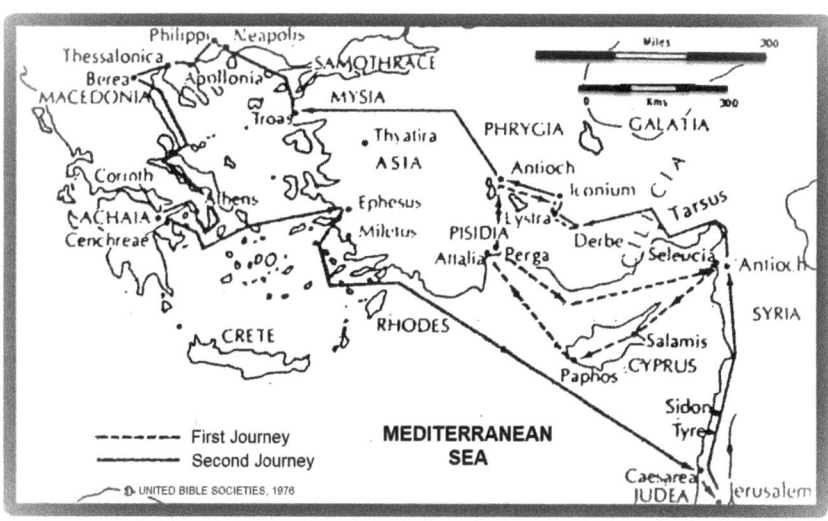

Lesson 74

Paul: God's Helper with Many Churches

> *Acts 13:47 (page _____ in the New Testament): For this is the commandment that the Lord has given us: "I have made you a light for the Gentiles, so that all the world may be saved."*

1. **Paul preached repentance.**

    Acts 26:20 (page _____ in the New Testament): "First in Damascus and in Jerusalem and then in the whole country of Israel and among the Gentiles, I preached that they must repent of their sins and turn to God and do the things that would show they had repented."

2. **Paul continued his journeys.**

    Acts 15:36, 40-41 (page _____ in the New Testament): Some time later Paul said to Barnabas, "Let us go back and visit our brothers in every town where we preached the word of the Lord, and let us find out how they are getting along". . . . Paul chose Silas and left, commended by the believers to the care of the Lord's grace. He went through Syria and Cilicia, strengthening the churches.

3. **The churches grew.**

    Acts 16:5 (page _____ in the New Testament): So the churches were made stronger in the faith and grew in numbers every day.

Part V: The People God Chose to Start and Build His Church

4. Paul and Silas obeyed God's instructions.

Acts 16:9-12 (page _____ in the New Testament): That night Paul had a vision in which he saw a Macedonian standing and begging him, "Come over to Macedonia and help us!" As soon as Paul had this vision, we got ready to leave for Macedonia, because we decided that God had called us to preach the Good News to the people there. We left by ship from Troas and sailed straight across to Samothrace, and the next day to Neapolis. From there we went inland to Philippi, a city of the first district of Macedonia; it is also a Roman colony. We spent several days there.

5. Paul and Silas shared the Good News about Jesus. A woman named Lydia believed the Good News.

Acts 16:13-15 (page _____ in the New Testament): On the Sabbath we went out of the city to the riverside, where we thought there would be a place where Jews gathered for prayer. We sat down and talked to the women who gathered there. One of those who heard us was Lydia from Thyatira, who was a dealer in purple cloth. She was a woman who worshiped God, and the Lord opened her mind to pay attention to what Paul was saying. After she and the people of her house had been baptized, she invited us, "Come and stay in my house if you have decided that I am a true believer in the Lord." And she persuaded us to go.

6. Paul and Silas were persecuted for preaching the Good News about Jesus.

Acts 16:23-24 (page _____ in the New Testament): After a severe beating, they were thrown into jail, and the jailer was ordered to lock them up tight. Upon receiving this order, the jailer threw them into the inner cell and fastened their feet between heavy blocks of wood.

Lesson 75

Paul Told How to Be Saved from Eternal Death to Eternal Life

Ephesians 2: 8-9 (page _____ in the New Testament): For it is by God's grace that you have been saved through faith. It is not the result of your own efforts, but God's gift, so that no one can boast about it.

Key words of Christians:

> GRACE: God's gift of love through Jesus Christ.
>
> FAITH: My acceptance into my life of God's gift of love through Jesus Christ.
>
> SALVATION: Peace with God because I have accepted into my life God's gift of love through Jesus Christ.

1. **God's plan is to love everyone and for everyone to love Him.**

    Romans 5:8 (page _____ in the New Testament): But God has shown us how much He loves us—it was while we were still sinners that Christ died for us!

2. **Everyone is separated from God by sin.**

    Romans 2:23 (page _____ in the New Testament): Everyone has sinned and is far away from God's saving presence.

Sin is choosing my way instead of God's way.

Sin is thinking my thoughts instead of God's thoughts.

Sin is saying my words instead of God's words.

Sin is doing my deeds instead of God's deeds.

Sin is putting myself where God should be.

3. **Sin brings eternal separation from God.**

    2 Thessalonians 1:9 (page _____ in the New Testament): They will suffer the punishment of eternal destruction, separated from the presence of the Lord and from His glorious might.

4. **Jesus Christ who died on the cross for our sin gives eternal life with God.**

    1 Timothy 2:5-6 (page _____ in the New Testament): For there is one God, and there is One who brings God and mankind together, the man Christ Jesus, who gave Himself to redeem all mankind. That was the proof at the right time that God wants everyone to be saved.

5. **Everyone who accepts (receives) God's gift of love through Jesus Christ is saved to eternal life with God.**

    Romans 10:9-10 (page _____ in the New Testament): If you confess that Jesus is Lord and believe that God raised Him from death, you will be saved. For it is by our faith that we are put right with God; it is by our confession that we are saved.

6. **Each person must choose God's way—eternal life—or choose his own way—eternal death.**

    If you really want Jesus to come into your life, pray this prayer:

    > *Dear Lord Jesus, please come into my life and be my Savior and Lord. Please forgive my sin and give me Your gift of eternal life.*
    > *Thank You, Jesus. Amen.*

    If you prayed this prayer sincerely, you NOW have eternal life!

    Romans 10:13 (page _____ in the New Testament): As the Scripture says, "Everyone who calls out to the Lord for help will be saved."

God's Plan of Love

7. Paul and Silas were prisoners in jail. They continued to preach the Good News about Jesus.

   i. Paul and Silas praised God in jail.

   Acts 16:25 (page _____ in the New Testament): About midnight Paul and Silas were praying and singing hymns to God, and the other prisoners were listening to them.

   ii. There was a big earthquake.

   Acts 16:26 (page _____ in the New Testament): Suddenly there was a violent earthquake, which shook the prison to its foundations. At once all the doors opened, and the chains fell off all the prisoners.

   iii. The jailer thought the prisoners had escaped.

   Acts 16:27 (page _____ in the New Testament): The jailer woke up, and when he saw the prison doors open, he thought that the prisoners had escaped; so he pulled out his sword and was about to kill himself.

   iv. *Acts 16:28 (page _____ in the New Testament): Paul shouted at the top of his voice, "Don't harm yourself! We are still here!"*

   v. *Acts 16:29-30 (page _____ in the New Testament): The jailer called for a light, rushed in, and fell trembling at the feet of Paul and Silas. Then he led them out and asked, "Sirs, what must I do to be saved?"*

   vi. Paul and Silas told the jailer how to be saved.

   Acts 16:31-32 (page _____ in the New Testament): They answered, "Believe in the Lord, Jesus, and you will be saved—you and your family." Then they preached the Word of the Lord to him and to all the others in the house.

   vii. The jailer believed the Good News about Jesus.

   Acts 16:33-34 (page _____ in the New Testament): At that very hour of the night the jailer took them and washed their wounds; and he and all his family were baptized at once. Then he took Paul and Silas up into his house and gave them some food to eat. He and his family were filled with joy, because they now believed in God.

---

2 Timothy 1:11-13 (page _____ in the New Testament): God has appointed me as an apostle and teacher to proclaim the Good News, and it is for this reason that I suffer these things. But I am still full of confidence, because I know Whom I have trusted, and I am sure that He is able to keep safe until that Day what He has entrusted to me. Hold firmly to the true words that I taught you, as the example for you to follow, and remain in the faith and love that are ours in union with Christ Jesus.

Lesson 76

Paul Told Christians How to Praise God

> *1 Thessalonians 5:16-18 (page _____ in the New Testament): Be joyful always, pray at all times, be thankful in all circumstances. This is what God wants from you in your life in union with Christ Jesus.*

1. **Paul told Christians to rejoice.**

   Philippians 4:4 (page _____ in the New Testament): May you always be joyful in your union with the Lord. I say it again: rejoice!

   i. Praise is words and actions.

      Colossians 3:16-17 (page _____ in the New Testament): Christ's message in all its richness must live in your hearts. Teach and instruct one another with all wisdom. Sing psalms, hymns, and sacred songs; sing to God with thanksgiving in your hearts. Everything you do or say, then, should be done in the name of the Lord Jesus, as you give thanks through Him to God the Father.

   ii. Paul told Christians to praise God, always.

      Ephesians 5:19-20 (page _____ in the New Testament): Speak to one another with the words of psalms, hymns, and sacred songs; sing hymns and psalms to the Lord with praise in your hearts. In the name of our Lord Jesus Christ, always give thanks for everything to God the Father.

   iii. Paul praised God in his time of trouble.

      Acts 16:25 (page _____ in the New Testament): About midnight Paul and Silas were praying and singing hymns to God, and the other prisoners were listening to them.

iv. Praise is obedience.

Psalm 50:14 (page _____ in the Old Testament): Let the giving of thanks be your sacrifice to God, and give the Almighty all that you promised.

Hebrews 13:15 (page _____ in the New Testament): Let us, then, always offer praise to God as our sacrifice through Jesus, which is the offering presented by lips that confess Him as Lord.

2. **Paul told Christians to pray with thanksgiving.**

   Philippians 4:6 (page _____ in the New Testament): Don't worry about anything, but in all your prayers ask God for what you need, always asking Him with a thankful heart.

3. **Paul told Christians they could have peace in their hearts through praise and thanksgiving.**

   Philippians 4:7 (page _____ in the New Testament): And God's peace, which is far beyond human understanding, will keep your hearts and minds safe in union with Christ Jesus.

4. **Paul told Christians the way to be able to praise God.**

   Philippians 4:8 (page _____ in the New Testament): In conclusion, my brothers, fill your minds with those things that are good and that deserve praise: things that are true, noble, right, pure, lovely, and honorable.

5. **Paul told Christians to obey God.**

   Philippians 4:9 (page _____ in the New Testament): Put into practice what you learned and received from me, both from my words and from my actions. And the God who gives us peace will be with you.

Other Psalms of praise that you can read from your Bible:

Psalm 98 (page _____ in the Old Testament)

Psalm 100 (page _____ in the Old Testament)

Psalm 113:1-4 (page _____ in the Old Testament)

Psalm 145–Psalm 150 (page _____ in the Old Testament)

Lesson 77

Paul Described Christian Love

Galatians 2:20 (page _____ in the New Testament): So that it is no longer I who live, but it is Christ who lives in me. This life that I live now, I live by faith in the Son of God, who loved me and gave His life for me.

1. **LOVE is the Christian reason for doing good things.**

   1 Corinthians 13:1-3 (page _____ in the New Testament): I may be able to speak the languages of men and even of angels but if I have no love, my speech is no more than a noisy gong or a clanging bell. I may have the gift of inspired preaching; I may have all knowledge and understand all secrets; I may have all the faith needed to move mountains—but if I have no love, I am nothing. I may give away everything I have, and even give up my body to be burned—but if I have no love, this does me no good.

2. **LOVE: This Scripture is from 1 Corinthians 13:4-7 (page _____ in the New Testament):**

   LOVE is patient and kind.

   LOVE is not jealous.

   LOVE is not conceited.

   LOVE is not proud.

   LOVE is not ill-mannered.

   LOVE is not selfish.

   LOVE is not irritable.

   LOVE does not keep a record of wrongs.

God's Plan of Love

LOVE is not happy with evil.

LOVE is happy with the truth.

LOVE never gives up.

LOVE is faith.

LOVE is hope.

LOVE is patient.

LOVE NEVER fails.

3. **LOVE is eternal (forever).**

   1 Corinthians 13:8-10 (page _____ in the New Testament): Love is eternal. There are inspired messages, but they are temporary; there are gifts of speaking in strange tongues, but they will cease; there is knowledge, but it will pass. For our gifts of knowledge and of inspired messages are only partial; but when what is perfect comes, then what is partial will disappear.

4. **LOVE is mature.**

   1 Corinthians 13:11-12 (page _____ in the New Testament): When I was child, my speech, feelings, and thinking were all those of a child; now that I am a man, I have no more use for childish ways. What we see now is like a dim image in a mirror; then we shall see face-to-face. What I know now is only partial; then it will be complete—as complete as God's knowledge of me.

5. **LOVE is true caring for God and man because God loves us and lives in us.**

   1 Corinthians 13:13 (page _____ in the New Testament): Meanwhile these three remain: faith, hope, and love; and the greatest of these is love.

   > *John 13:34-35 (page _____ in the New Testament): Jesus said, "I give you a new commandment: love one another. As I have loved you, so you must love one another. If you have love for one another, then everyone will know that you are my disciples."*

Lesson 78

Paul Told Christians How to Live a Life in God's Service

> *Romans 12:1-2 (page _____ in the New Testament): So then, my brothers, because of God's great mercy to us I appeal to you: Offer yourselves as a living sacrifice to God, dedicated to His service and pleasing to Him. This is the true worship that you should offer. Do not conform yourselves to the standards of this world, but let God transform you inwardly by a complete change of your mind. Then you will be able to know the will of God—what is good and is pleasing to Him and is perfect.*

1. **Paul told Christians WHY they should live a life in God's service.**

    Romans 12:1a (page _____ in the New Testament): So then, my brothers, BECAUSE OF GOD'S GREAT MERCY to us, I appeal to you. . . .

2. **Paul told Christians HOW they could live a life in God's service.**

    Romans 12:1b (page _____ in the New Testament): OFFER YOURSELVES as a living sacrifice to God, dedicated to His service and pleasing to Him. This is the true worship that you should offer.

    i. Jesus' death on the cross was the sacrifice for our sin.

        Hebrews 9:12 (page _____ in the New Testament): When Christ went through the tent and entered once and for all into the Most Holy Place, He did not take the blood of goats and bulls to offer as a sacrifice; rather, He took His own blood and obtained eternal salvation for us.

God's Plan of Love

ii. God wants Christians to be a LIVING SACRIFICE. A living sacrifice is a LIFE IN GOD'S SERVICE.

Hebrews 9:14 (page _____ in the New Testament): Since this is true, how much more is accomplished by the blood of Christ! Through the eternal Spirit He offered Himself as a perfect sacrifice to God. His blood will purify our consciences from useless rituals, so that we may serve the living God.

iii. God helps Christians live a life in God's service.

Romans 12:1 (page _____ in the New Testament): Do not conform yourselves to the standards of this world; but LET GOD TRANSFORM YOU inwardly by a complete change of your mind. Then you will be able to know the will of God—what is good and is pleasing to Him and is perfect.

3. **Paul gave Christians INSTRUCTIONS on how to live a life in God's service every day:**

   i. *Romans 12:3-21 (page _____ in the New Testament): With Christians . . . We have many parts in one body, and all these parts have different functions. In the same way, though we are many, we are one body in union with Christ, and we are all joined to each other as different parts of one body.*

   Do not think of yourself more highly than you should.

   Be modest in your thinking, and judge yourself according to the amount of faith God has given you.

   Love must be completely sincere. Love one another warmly as Christian brothers.

   Be eager to show respect for one another.

   Serve the Lord with a heart full of devotion. Share your belongings with your needy fellow Christians.

   ii. With all people . . . *Work hard and do not be lazy. Open your home to strangers.*

   Be happy with those who are happy. Weep with those who weep. Have the same concern for everyone.

   Do not be proud, but accept humble duties. Do not think of yourselves as wise.

   Try to do what everyone considers to be good.

   Do everything possible on your part to live in peace with everybody.

   iii. With your enemies . . . *If someone has done you wrong, do not repay him a wrong.*

> *Never take revenge, my friends, but instead let God's anger do it. For the Scripture says, "I will take revenge, I will pay back," says the Lord.*
>
> *The Scripture says, "If your enemy is hungry, feed him; if he is thirsty, give him drink; for by doing this you will make him burn with shame."*

    iv. With your troubles . . . *Let your hope keep you joyful, be patient in your trouble, pray at all times.*

    v. With evil in the world . . . *Hate what is evil, hold on to what is good. Do not let evil defeat you; conquer evil with good.*

Galatians 2:20 (page _____ in the New Testament): It is no longer I who live, but it is Christ who lives in me. This life that I live now, I live by faith in the Son of God Who loved me and gave His life for me.

2 Corinthians 5:17 (page _____ in the New Testament): When anyone is joined to Christ, he is a new being; the old is gone, the new has come.

These words of Paul continue to tell Christians today how to live a life in God's service. A life lived in God's service gives Christians:

> *Galatians 5:22-23a (page _____ in the New Testament): . . . love, joy, peace, patience, kindness, goodness, faithfulness, humility, and self control.*

Lesson 79

Paul Told That the Church Is the Body of Christ—All the Believers in Jesus Christ

> *1 Corinthians 12:27 (page _____ in the New Testament): All of you are Christ's body, and each one is a part of it.*

The Bible gives different word pictures to tell what the church is. One picture is a body with Christ as the head.

Colossians 1:17-18a (page _____ in the New Testament): Christ existed before all things, and in union with Him all things have their proper place. He is the head of His body, the church. . . .

1. **The body of Christ (the church) is made up of different kinds of people.**

   1 Corinthians 12:12-13 (page _____ in the New Testament): Christ is like a single body, which has many parts; it is still one body, even though it is made up of different parts. In the same way, all of us, whether Jews or Gentiles, whether slaves or free, have been baptized into the one body by the same Spirit, and we have all been given the one Spirit to drink.

2. **The physical body has many parts. Each part of the physical body has a special job to do.**

   1 Corinthians 12:14-24a (page _____ in the New Testament): For the body itself is not made up of only one part, but of many parts. If the foot were to say, "Because I am not a hand, I don't belong to the body," that would not keep it from being a part of the body. And if the ear were to say, "Because I am not an eye, I don't belong to the body," that would not keep it from being a part of the body. If the whole body were just an eye, how could it hear? And if it were only an ear, how could it smell? As it is, however, God put every different part in the body just as He wanted it to be. There would not be a body if it were all only one part! As it is, there are many parts but one body. So then, the eye cannot say to the hand, "I don't need you!" Nor can the head say to the feet, "Well, I don't need you!" On the contrary, we cannot do without the parts of the body that seem to be weaker; and those parts that we think aren't worth very much are the ones which we treat with greater care; while the parts of the body which don't look very nice are treated with special modesty, which the more beautiful parts do not need.

3. **All the parts must work together to have a healthy physical body.**

    1 Corinthians 12:24b-26 (page _____ in the New Testament): God Himself has put the body together in such a way as to give greater honor to those parts that need it. And so there is no division in the body, but all its different parts have the same concern for one another. If one part of the body suffers, all the other parts suffer with it; if one part is praised, all the other parts share its happiness.

4. **The parts of the body of Christ (the church) must work together to have a healthy spiritual body.**

    1 Corinthians 12:27-30 (page _____ in the New Testament): All of you are Christ's body, and each one is a part of it. In the church God has put all in place; in the first place apostles, in the second place prophets, and in the third place teachers; then those who perform miracles, followed by those who are given the power to heal or to help others or to direct them or to speak in strange tongues. They are not all apostles or prophets or teachers. Not everyone has the power to work miracles or to heal diseases or to speak in strange tongues or to explain what is said.

The way the body of Christ (the church) works together best is in love. Read from your Bible 1 Corinthians 13 (page _____ in the New Testament).

> *1 Corinthians 14:1a (page _____ in the New Testament): It is love, then, that you should strive for. . . .*

Lesson 80

Jesus Is Coming Again

> *1 Thessalonians 4:14 (page _____ in the New Testament): We believe that Jesus died and rose again, and so we believe that God will take back with Jesus those who have died believing in Him.*

1. **Jesus told His disciples that He was going to heaven to be with His Father. Jesus promised that He would come back to earth.**

    John 14:1-4 (page _____ in the New Testament): "Do not be worried and upset," Jesus told them. "Believe in God and believe also in Me. There are many rooms in My Father's house, and I am going to prepare a place for you. I would not tell you this if it were not so. And after I go and prepare a place for you, I will come back and take you to Myself, so that you will be where I am. You know the way that leads to the place where I am going."

2. **Jesus told His disciples the only way to get to the Father.**

    John 14:5-7 (page _____ in the New Testament): Thomas said to Him, "Lord, we do not know where You are going; so how can we know the way to get there?" Jesus answered him, "I am the Way, the Truth, and the Life; no one goes to the Father except by Me. Now that you have known Me," He said to them, "you will know My Father also, and from now on you do know Him and you have seen Him."

3. **No one knows when Jesus will come again.**

    Matthew 24:36 (page _____ in the New Testament): "No one knows, however, when that day and hour will come—neither the angels in heaven nor the Son; the Father alone knows."

Luke 12:40 (page _____ in the New Testament): "And you, too, must be ready, because the Son of Man will come at an hour when you are not expecting Him."

4. The Bible tells how Jesus is coming again.

Matthew 24:29-31 (page _____ in the New Testament): "Soon after the trouble of those days, the sun will grow dark, the moon will no longer shine, the stars will fall from heaven, and the powers in space will be driven from their courses. Then the sign of the Son of Man will appear in the sky; and all the peoples of earth will weep as they see the Son of Man coming on the clouds of heaven with power and great glory. The great trumpet will sound, and He will send out His angels to the four corners of the earth, and they will gather His chosen people from one end of the world to the other."

1 Thessalonians 4:15-18 (page _____ in the New Testament): What we are teaching you now is the Lord's teaching: we who are alive on the day the Lord comes will not go ahead of those who have died. There will be the shout of command, the archangel's voice, the sound of God's trumpet, and the LORD HIMSELF will come down from heaven. Those who have died believing in Christ will rise to life first; then we who are living at that time will be gathered up along with them in the clouds to meet the LORD in the air! And so we will always be with the LORD. So then, encourage one another with these words.

Revelation 22:7, 17b, 20b, 21 (page _____ in the New Testament): "Listen!" says Jesus, "I am coming soon! Happy are those who obey the prophetic words in this book!" . . . Come, whoever is thirsty; accept the water of life as a gift, whoever wants it. . . . So be it. Come Lord Jesus! May the grace of the Lord Jesus be with everyone.

Part VI:

The Bible Teaches Us about Prayer

Lesson 81

What Is Prayer?

Prayer is communication between God and people.

Jeremiah 33:2-3 (page _____ in the Old Testament): The LORD, who made the earth, who formed it and set it in place, spoke to me. He whose name is the LORD said, "Call to Me, and I will answer you; I will tell you wonderful and marvelous things that you know nothing about."

1. **God showed His love for all people.**

   1 John 4:10 (page _____ in the New Testament): This is what love is: it is not that we have loved God, but that He loved us and sent His Son to be the means by which our sins are forgiven.

2. **Some people choose to respond to God's love.**

   John 1:10-12 (page _____ in the New Testament): The Word was in the world, and though God made the world through Him, yet the world did not recognize Him. He came to His own country, but His own people did not receive Him. Some, however, did receive Him and believed in Him, so He gave them the right to become God's children.

3. **Prayer is a special way people express love for God.**

   In the Old Testament God says, "Love the LORD your God with all your heart, with all your soul, and with all your strength" (Deuteronomy 6:5, page _____ in the Old Testament).

God's Plan of Love

In the New Testament Jesus says, "Love the Lord your God with all your heart, with all your soul, with all your mind, and with all your strength" (Mark 12:30, page _____ in the New Testament).

> *Thanksgiving is prayer.*
>
> *Praise is prayer.*
>
> *Obedience is prayer.*

1 Thessalonians 5:16-18 (page _____ in the New Testament): Be joyful always, pray at all times, be thankful in all circumstances. This is what God wants from you in your life in union with Christ Jesus.

4. **Prayer is a special way people tell God about their needs.**

    Psalm 5:1-3 (page _____ in the Old Testament): Listen to my words, O LORD, and hear my sighs. Listen to my cry for help, my God and King! I pray to You, O Lord; You hear my voice in the morning; at sunrise I offer my prayer and wait for Your answer.

5. **Prayer is a special way God teaches people about His love.**

    Isaiah 43:1-3a, 4b-5a (page _____ in the Old Testament): The LORD who created you says, "Do not be afraid—I will save you. I have called you by name—you are mine. When you pass through deep waters, I will be with you; your troubles will not overwhelm you. When you pass through fire, you will not be burned; the hard trials that come will not hurt you. For I am the LORD your God. . . . because you are precious to Me and because I love you and give you honor. Do not be afraid—I am with you!"

Prayer is getting to know God!

Part VI: The Bible Teaches Us about Prayer

Lesson 82

Why Do People Pray?

> *Jeremiah 33:2-3 (page _____ in the Old Testament): The LORD, who made the earth, who formed it and set it in place, spoke to me. He whose name is the LORD said, "Call to Me, and I will answer you; I will tell you wonderful and marvelous things that you know nothing about."*

1. **People pray because they want to know God.**

   Ephesians 3:17-18 (page _____ in the New Testament): I pray that Christ will make His home in your hearts through faith. I pray that you may have your roots and foundation in love, so that you, together with all God's people, may have the power to understand how broad and long, how high and deep, is Christ's love.

2. **People pray because they want to know God better.**

   Philippians 3:10 (page _____ in the New Testament): All I want is to know Christ and to experience the power of His resurrection, to share in His sufferings and become like Him in His death.

   Ephesians 3:19 (page _____ in the New Testament): Yes, may you come to know His love—although it can never be fully known—and so be completely filled with the very nature of God.

3. **People pray:**

   i. To glorify/praise God.

   Ephesians 1:6 (page _____ in the New Testament): Let us praise God for His glorious grace, for the free gift He gave us in His dear Son!

God's Plan of Love

    ii. To feel God's presence.

        Psalm 116:1-2 (page _____ in the Old Testament): I love the LORD, because He hears me; He listens to my prayers. He listens to me every time I call to Him.

        Psalm 23 (page _____ in the Old Testament): The LORD is my Shepherd; I have everything I need. He lets me rest in fields of green grass and leads me to quiet pools of fresh water. He gives me new strength. He guides me in the right paths, as He has promised. Even if I go through the deepest darkness, I will not be afraid, LORD, for You are with me. Your Shepherd's rod and staff protect me. You prepare a banquet for me, where all my enemies can see me; you welcome me as an honored guest and fill my cup to the brim. I know that Your goodness and love will be with me all my life; and Your house will be my home as long as I live.

    iii. For comfort in time of need.

        2 Corinthians 1:3-4 (page _____ in the New Testament): Let us give thanks to the God and Father of our Lord Jesus Christ, the merciful Father, the God from whom all help comes! He helps us in all our troubles, so that we are able to help others who have all kinds of troubles, using the same help that we ourselves have received from God.

    iv. To experience God's forgiveness.

        Psalm 51:1-4, 7, 9-10 (page _____ in the Old Testament): Be merciful to me, O God, because of Your constant love. Because of Your great mercy wipe away my sins! Wash away all my evil and make me clean from my sin! I recognize my faults; I am always conscious of my sins. I have sinned against You—only against You—and done what You consider evil. So You are right in judging me; You are justified in condemning me. . . . Remove my sin, and I will be clean; wash me, and I will be whiter than snow. . . . Create a pure heart in me, O God, and put a new and loyal spirit in me.

    v. To know God's guidance and direction.

        Psalm 25:4-5 (page _____ in the Old Testament): Teach me Your ways, O LORD; make them known to me. Teach me to live according to Your truth, for You are my God, who saves me. I always trust in You.

        Psalm 32:8 (page _____ in the Old Testament): The LORD says, "I will teach you the way you should go; I will instruct you and advise you."

    vi. To resist temptation.

Part VI: The Bible Teaches Us about Prayer

Ephesians 6:13, 18 (page _____ in the New Testament): So put on God's armor now! Then when the evil day comes, you will be able to resist the enemy's attacks; and after fighting to the end, you will still hold your ground . . . Do all this in prayer, asking for God's help. Pray on every occasion, as the Spirit leads. For this reason keep alert and never give up; pray always for all God's people.

Jeremiah 29:12-13 (page _____ in the Old Testament): God said, "Then you will call to Me. You will come and pray to Me, and I will answer you. You will seek Me, and you will find Me because you will seek Me with all your heart."

Let us . . . praise God's glory!

God's Plan of Love

Lesson 83

How Do People Pray?

> *Jeremiah 33:2-3 (page _____ in the Old Testament): The LORD, who made the earth, who formed it and set it in place, spoke to me. He whose name is the LORD said, "Call to Me, and I will answer you; I will tell you wonderful and marvelous things that you know nothing about."*

1. **People pray with words:**

   with their own words,

   with words of other people,

   with words of hymns,

   with words of the Bible.

   Psalm 19:14 (page _____ in the Old Testament): May my words and my thoughts be acceptable to You, O LORD, my Refuge and my Redeemer.

2. **People pray without words. People pray with:**

   thoughts,

   attitudes,

   feelings,

   actions.

   Romans 8:26-27 (page _____ in the New Testament): In the same way the Spirit also comes to help us, weak as we are. For we do not know how we ought to pray; the Spirit Himself pleads with God for us in groans that words cannot express. And God, who sees into our hearts, knows what the thought of the Spirit is; because the Spirit pleads with God on behalf of His people and in accordance with His will.

3. **People pray alone.**

   Matthew 6:6 (page _____ in the New Testament): "But when you pray, go to your room, close the door, and pray to your Father, who is unseen. And your Father, who sees what you do in private, will reward you."

4. **People pray with others in church, in groups, and in the home.**

   Matthew 18:20 (page _____ in the New Testament): "For where two or three come together in My name, I am there with them "

5. **People pray at times of joy, of sadness, and of celebration.**

   Ephesians 6:18 (page _____ in the New Testament): Do all this in prayer, asking for God's help. Pray on every occasion, as the Spirit leads. For this reason keep alert and never give up; pray always for all God's people.

People can pray any time, anywhere, and any place!

Lesson 84

What Are Some Ways to Pray?

Jeremiah 33:2-3 (page _____ in the Old Testament): The LORD, who made the earth, who formed it and set it in place, spoke to me. He whose name is the LORD said, "Call to Me, and I will answer you; I will tell you wonderful and marvelous things that you know nothing about."

1. **People pray in many ways:**

    i. Thanksgiving: thanking God for all things.

    ii. Confession: telling God all their sins and asking His forgiveness.

    iii. Praise: telling God that He is great, glorious, wonderful, marvelous, and that they love Him.

    iv. Petition: asking God for all their needs.

    v. Intercession: praying for all people:

    family,

    friends,

    people in authority,

    enemies.

    vi. Guidance: asking God to help them obey Him in every way, every day.

2. **Jesus taught a way to pray.**

    Matthew 6:9-13 (page _____ in the New Testament):

    "This, then, is how you should pray:

'Our Father in heaven: May Your holy name be honored;

May Your Kingdom come; May Your will be done on earth as it is in heaven.

Give us today the food we need.

Forgive us the wrongs we have done, as we forgive the wrongs that others have done to us.

Do not bring us to hard testing, but keep us safe from the Evil One.'"

Today people pray this prayer. People also pray their own prayers.

Lesson 85

Does God Answer Prayer?

Jeremiah 33:2-3 (page _____ in the Old Testament): The LORD, who made the earth, who formed it and set it in place, spoke to me. He whose name is the LORD said, "Call to Me, and I will answer you; I will tell you wonderful and marvelous things that you know nothing about."

1. **God does answer prayer.**

Isaiah 58:9 (page _____ in the Old Testament): When you pray, I will answer you. When you call to Me, I will respond.

2. **Sometimes God's answer to prayer is, "Yes."**

Matthew 7:7-11 (page _____ in the New Testament): "Ask, and you will receive; seek, and you will find; knock, and the door will be opened to you. For everyone who asks will receive, and anyone who seeks will find, and the door will be opened to him who knocks. Would any of you who are fathers give your son a stone when he asks for bread? Or would you give him a snake when he asks for a fish? As bad as you are, you know how to give good things to your children. How much more, then, will your Father in heaven give good things to those who ask Him!"

3. **Sometimes God's answer to prayer is, "No." God's answer is always best!**

Paul: 2 Corinthians 12:8-10 (page _____ in the New Testament): Three times I prayed to the Lord about this and asked Him to take it away. But His answer was: "My grace is all you need, for My power is greatest when you are weak." I am most happy, then, to be proud of my weaknesses, in order to feel the protection of Christ's power over me. I am *content with weaknesses, insults, hardships, persecutions, and difficulties for Christ's sake. For when I am weak, then I am strong.*

Luke 22:42-43 (page _____ in the New Testament): Jesus: "Father," He said, "If You will, take this cup of suffering away from Me. Not My will, however, but Your will be done." An angel from heaven appeared to Him and strengthened Him.

4. Sometimes God's answer to prayer is, "Wait!"

Habakkuk 2:3c (page _____ in the Old Testament): "It (the answer) may seem slow in coming, but wait for it. . . ."

> *Romans 8:28 (page _____ in the New Testament): We know that in all things God works for good with those who love Him, those whom He has called according to His purpose.*

Lesson 86

What Helps Christians Pray?

Jeremiah 33:2-3 (page _____ in the Old Testament): The LORD, who made the earth, who formed it and set it in place, spoke to me. He whose name is the LORD said, "Call to Me, and I will answer you; I will tell you wonderful and marvelous things that you know nothing about."

For Christians, prayer is communication with God through Jesus Christ.

1. **A Christian is a person who chooses God's way. Choosing God's way is accepting Jesus Christ as Saviour.**

   Acts 16:31b (page _____ in the New Testament): "Believe in the Lord Jesus, and you will be saved."

2. **The Bible tells Christians to pray.**

   Ephesians 6:18 (page _____ in the New Testament): Do all this in prayer, asking for God's help. Pray on every occasion, as the Spirit leads. For this reason keep alert and never give up; pray always for all God's people.

   1 Thessalonians 5:16-18 (page _____ in the New Testament): Be joyful always, pray at all times, be thankful in all circumstances. This is what God wants from you in your life in union with Christ Jesus.

   Christians learn to pray by praying.
   Christians can talk to God anywhere, at any time, in any language.
   Christians can talk to God with words they use every day.
   Christians can tell God just what they think.
   Christians can tell God just how they feel.

3. What are some helps and hindrances to praying?

Helps	Hindrances
Forgiving spirit—*Luke 23:34 (page _____ in the New Testament): Jesus said, "Forgive them, Father! They don't know what they are doing."*	**Unforgiving spirit**—*Mark 11:25 (page _____ in the New Testament): "And when you stand and pray, forgive anything you may have against anyone, so that your Father in heaven will forgive the wrongs you have done."* *Matthew 5:23-24 (page _____ in the New Testament): "So if you are about to offer your gift to God at the altar and there you remember that your brother has something against you, leave your gift there in front of the altar, go at once and make peace with your brother, and then come back and offer your gift to God."*
Confessed sin—*1 John 1:8-10 (page _____ in the New Testament): If we say that we have no sin, we deceive ourselves, and there is no truth in us. But if we confess our sins to God, He will keep His promise and do what is right: He will forgive us our sins and purify us from all our wrongdoing. If we say that we have not sinned, we make a liar out of God, and His Word is not in us.*	**Unconfessed sin**—*Psalm 66:18 (page _____ in the Old Testament): If I had ignored my sins, the Lord would not have listened to me.*
Obeying God—*1 Peter 1:14 (page _____ in the New Testament): Be obedient to God, and do not allow your lives to be shaped by those desires you had when you were still ignorant.*	**Disobeying God**—*Ephesians 2:1 (page _____ in the New Testament): In the past you were spiritually dead because of your disobedience and sins.* *Titus 3:3a (page _____ in the New Testament): For we ourselves were once foolish, disobedient, and wrong.*

Prayer is getting to know God through Jesus Christ.

Prayer is realizing my need for Jesus Christ.

Prayer is recognizing His presence in my life.

> *John 10:10b (page _____ in the New Testament): Jesus said, "I have come in order that you might have life—life in all its fullness."*

God's Plan of Love

Lesson 87

How Do I Pray?

> *Jeremiah 33:2-3 (page _____ in the Old Testament): The LORD, who made the earth, who formed it and set it in place, spoke to me. He whose name is the LORD said, "Call to Me, and I will answer you; I will tell you wonderful and marvelous things that you know nothing about."*

Prayer is a special way to express my love for God.

Prayer is a special way to tell God my needs.

Prayer is a special way God teaches me His love.

THANKSGIVING: thanking God for all things.

Dear God, thank You for… _____

_____

_____

_____

CONFESSION: telling God all of my sins and asking His forgiveness.

Father in Heaven, I know I have thought bad things, I have said bad things, and I have done bad things. Please forgive me for… _____

_____

_____

_____

Part VI: The Bible Teaches Us about Prayer

PRAISE: telling God that He is great, glorious, wonderful, marvelous, and that I love Him.

God, you are… _____

_____

_____

_____

PETITION: asking God for all my needs.

Father, I need… _____

_____

_____

_____

INTERCESSION: praying for all people: my family, my friends, for people in authority, and for my enemies.

Dear Father in Heaven, I pray for… _____

_____

_____

_____

GUIDANCE: asking God to help me obey Him in every way, every day.

Dear Lord, I need Your help for… _____

_____

_____

_____

Prayer is getting to know God through Jesus Christ.

Prayer is realizing my need for Jesus Christ.

Prayer is recognizing His presence in my life.

For Christians, prayer is communication with God through Jesus Christ.

> *Ephesians 3:17-18 (page _____ in the New Testament): I pray that Christ will make His home in your hearts through faith. I pray that you may have your roots and foundation in love, so that you, together with all God's people, may have the power to understand how broad and long, how high and deep, is Christ's love.*

www.ingramcontent.com/pod-product-compliance
Lightning Source LLC
Chambersburg PA
CBHW081834170426
43199CB00017B/2727